Olha Tatokhina (ed.)

Why Do They Kill Our People?

Russia's War Against Ukraine as Told by Ukrainians

Editor-in-Chief and with a preface by
Volodymyr Yermolenko

Ukrainian Voices

Collected by Andreas Umland

79   Olga Khomenko
     The Faraway Sky of Kyiv
     Ukrainians in the War
     With a foreword by Hiroaki Kuromiya
     ISBN 978-3-8382-2006-2

80   Daria Mattingly, Jonathon Vsetecka (eds.)
     The Holodomor in Global Perspective
     How the Famine in Ukraine Shaped the World
     ISBN 978-3-8382-1953-0

81   Olga Khomenko
     Ukrainians beyond Borders
     Nine Life Journeys Through the History of Eastern Europe
     With a foreword by Zbigniew Wojnowski
     ISBN 978-3-8382-2007-9

82   Mykhailo Minakov
     From Servant to Leader
     Chronicles of Ukraine under the Zelensky presidency, 2019–2024
     ISBN 978-3-8382-2002-4

83   Wolodymyr Hromov (ed.)
     A Ruined Home
     Sketches of War, 2022–2023
     ISBN 978-3-8382-2008-6

The book series "Ukrainian Voices" publishes English- and German-language monographs, edited volumes, document collections, and anthologies of articles authored and composed by Ukrainian politicians, intellectuals, activists, officials, researchers, and diplomats. The series' aim is to introduce Western and other audiences to Ukrainian explorations, deliberations and interpretations of historic and current, domestic, and international affairs. The purpose of these books is to make non-Ukrainian readers familiar with how some prominent Ukrainians approach, view and assess their country's development and position in the world. The series was founded, and the volumes are collected by Andreas Umland, Dr. phil. (FU Berlin), Ph. D. (Cambridge), Associate Professor of Politics at the Kyiv-Mohyla Academy and an Analyst in the Stockholm Centre for Eastern European Studies at the Swedish Institute of International Affairs.

Olha Tatokhina (ed.)

WHY DO THEY KILL OUR PEOPLE?

Russia's War Against Ukraine as Told by Ukrainians

Editor-in-Chief and with a preface by

Volodymyr Yermolenko

Bibliografische Information der Deutschen Nationalbibliothek
Die Deutsche Nationalbibliothek verzeichnet diese Publikation in der Deutschen Nationalbibliografie; detaillierte bibliografische Daten sind im Internet über http://dnb.d-nb.de abrufbar.

Bibliographic information published by the Deutsche Nationalbibliothek
The Deutsche Nationalbibliothek lists this publication in the Deutsche Nationalbibliografie; detailed bibliographic data are available on the Internet at http://dnb.d-nb.de.

Editor: Olha Tatokhina
Editor-in-Chief: Volodymyr Yermolenko
Illustrations: Serhiy Zakharov
Copy-editing: Joel Wasserman
Layout: Svitlana Nevdashchenko
Team lead: Alona Hryshko

Published with kind permission of Internews Ukraine, Kyiv.
Originally published by Dukh i Litera, Kyiv, 2024.

Supported by:

ISBN (Print): 978-3-8382-2056-7
ISBN (E-Book [PDF]): 978-3-8382-8056-1
© *ibidem*-Verlag, Hannover • Stuttgart 2024
Alle Rechte vorbehalten

Das Werk einschließlich aller seiner Teile ist urheberrechtlich geschützt. Jede Verwertung außerhalb der engen Grenzen des Urheberrechtsgesetzes ist ohne Zustimmung des Verlages unzulässig und strafbar. Dies gilt insbesondere für Vervielfältigungen, Übersetzungen, Mikroverfilmungen und elektronische Speicherformen sowie die Einspeicherung und Verarbeitung in elektronischen Systemen.

All rights reserved. No part of this publication may be reproduced, stored in or introduced into a retrieval system, or transmitted, in any form, or by any means (electronic, mechanical, photocopying, recording or otherwise) without the prior written permission of the publisher. Any person who commits any unauthorized act in relation to this publication may be liable to criminal prosecution and civil claims for damages.

Printed in the EU

Acknowledgments

We thank all those people who provided their stories for this book, for their courage. We mourn those who were killed by Russia and who will never speak to us again. We hail Ukraine's defenders for their courageous actions in saving Ukraine and the world from the inhuman cruelty of Putin's Russia.

We thank our partners from the Kharkiv Human Rights Protection Group for their work in documenting Russian war crimes and for helping us to collect some of the stories of this book. We are particularly grateful to KHPG director Yevhen Zakharov, as well as the group's documentors: Taras Zozulinskyi, Antonina Dembytska, Andrii Didenko, Taras Viychuk, Oleksandr Vasyliev, Denys Volokha, Oleksii Sydorenko, Mykola Tsipko, Bohdana Chernushenko, and Iryna Skachko.

We thank the National Democratic Institute for its support of our idea of collecting human stories and publishing this book. We also thank our other partners, in particular the International Renaissance Foundation, Internews Network, and USAID for supporting the work of UkraineWorld, in particular in collecting the human stories of Russia's war against Ukraine.

We thank the Internews Ukraine and UkraineWorld teams for their hard work on this publication, and we thank our friends from the Dukh I Litera publishing house for publishing this book.

Contents

PREFACE 12

Defending and Curing: Stories of Soldiers and Paramedics 15

    "I meet my friends in cemeteries." 20-year-old writer Oksana
became a soldier to defend her motherland 16

    "I have to be unbreakable." 19-year-old defender Ruslana
lost her leg to Russian shelling 18

    He will never meet his friends again. Ukrainian soldier Ihor
survived enemy fire but lost his comrades 20

    No happy birthday wishes. Ukrainian soldier Serhii
spends his birthday in the trenches 24

    "I'll be here and do my best."
Soldiers keep fighting through crushing fatigue 26

    This soldier lost his arms and a leg during the war.
Zakhar was seriously injured and is now undergoing treatment abroad 27

    Living without both legs. Oleksii is a veterinarian who joined
the army and was seriously injured in the war 29

    Volunteer doctors save the lives of the Ukrainian soldiers.
A mobile hospital provides medical assistance at the frontline 31

The Fragility of Life: Stories of Childbirth and Children Amidst War 35

    Childhood under fire. Valentyna's family fled the horrors of war 36

    An 8-month-old child was born under shelling.
Kateryna, his mother, tells their story 38

    Giving birth on Day 1. Yuliia's son was born on February 24, 2022, in Kyiv 40

    "Almost nothing is left of our city." Anna tells
the story of Lysychansk, where she recently had a baby 42

    "I had one goal." Olena fled the war with two small children 44

    With kids amidst missiles falling nearby. Yuliia evacuated
her three children through a torrent of missiles 47

    "We will no longer have the life we had before."
Yevheniia evacuated with her daughter due to continuous Russian shelling 51

    Saving her daughter from a city under fire.
The story of Svitlana from Kharkiv 53

In the Clutches of Grief: Stories of the Loss of Loved Ones 55

Tears of a Soldier's Widow. A letter from a wife left behind 56

Shattered Dreams and the Meaning of Life. The story
of Maryna Baliaba from Bucha, whose husband died in the war 57

"I want to take your hand and not let it go."
Alla's boyfriend was killed by a Russian shell 58

This father will never see his newborn daughter.
Nataliia lost her husband Vitalii 60

Russia killed Daria's husband and father of twins.
Artem, a Ukrainian soldier, fell in Lysychansk 62

"I am young, I am a widow."
Nadiia's husband was killed in the war. She tells their story 64

10-year-old Nastia was killed by the Russians.
The story of the Stoliuk family from a village near Kyiv 66

His wife was kidnapped and murdered by the Russians.
The story of Ihor from Trostianets 68

Surviving Atrocities: Tales of Life Under Russian Occupation 69

"People were kidnapped from streets and cafés."
Anastasiia from Berdiansk tells her story of occupation and evacuation 70

"The nights were the scariest for me." Life during the siege of Mariupol 72

"I will remember that night for the rest of my life."
Mariia and her child lived through Russian occupation and bombing 76

"Russians were shooting people at random."
Tetiana survived the occupation of Borodianka with her family 78

"We didn't have the medicines we needed."
Serhii survived the Russian occupation of Izium 80

"They put all the villagers in the school basement."
Anzhelika tells the story of Yahidne 82

"Russia is worse than a horde." Mykola survived
the Russian occupation of Moshchun 84

Surviving the bomb strike. The story of Larysa from Borodianka 86

Journeys to safety: Evacuation Chronicles 89

Bullets stuck in her body. Myroslava escaped
death while leaving Irpin with her daughter 90

Evacuating, returning home, and evacuating again.
Kateryna fled the war from Zaporizhzhia with her young son 94

"Children shouldn't live in fear." Tetiana left Kharkiv with her children 97

Meeting empathy and help in Poland.
Nadiia from Kyiv was evacuated to Poland with her children 99

"My cat is my hero." Nataliia managed to evacuate
from Mariupol with her old cat Marta. She tells her story 101

The occupiers' furious faces. The story of deacon Mykola,
whose family escaped Russian occupation 103

"People were knocking on the train door, begging to be let on."
Valentyna tells a story of her journey from Russian-shelled Kramatorsk 106

"People were buried in public squares, parks,
and next to their houses." Vira survived the apocalypse in Mariupol 108

Shattered Homes: Stories of Ruin From Russian Bombing 111

Russian missiles destroy apartments, but not the lust for life.
Ania from Kyiv lost her home to the Russian shelling and tells her story 112

"Son, they are bombing us!" The story of Mykola,
who survived the horrific assault on Kharkiv 115

"We don't have an apartment anymore." Kateryna
lost her home in Kharkiv after a Russian strike 117

"The Russians 'liberated' me from my own house."
The story of Ihor from Moshchun 119

A shell flew into the room, knocking out the wall and the window.
Hanna's apartment in Horenka was hit by Russian bombing 121

"I left my home in my trousers, boots, and a jacket."
The story of Petro from Moschun 123

"Dogs were pulling at human remains."
The story of Ninelle from Borodianka 125

Torment and Humiliation: Enduring Russian Brutality 127

The Russians would come to your home at 5 a.m.
Viktoriia describes searches in Russian-occupied Kherson 128

Beaten with a heating pipe. Vadym spent 110 days
in a Russian torture camp in Kupiansk 130

Bag on his head, string around his neck.
Vitalii survived Russian torture in Borodianka 133

PREFACE

This book is not for relaxation. It will not make you happier. It may leave you feeling anxious. It may spark insomnia. But it will show you things you need to see something important – dignity and resistance, but also cruelty and evil.

This is not a book which concerns itself with the beauty of words or metaphors. This is a book that has grown from the dark, blood- and tear-soaked soil of the Ukrainian experience during the war, from pain and courage, from fragility and mortality, and from hope and despair. It is a book of testimony.

This experience is painful. These stories are difficult to read. They were not decorated. Instead, the stories were kept as they were told, in very simple words.

These stories were told to us by Ukrainians who went through some of their people's worst days, through the hell forced upon them by Russia in another of Moscow's typical cruel and senseless wars.

There is a story of a child born on the day when the great war started. There is a story of a child who was killed and had to be buried three times.

There are stories of soldiers who will live the rest of their lives without legs or arms. Stories of those who will never see their homes again, or whose cities have been destroyed and occupied.

There are stories of long and painful journeys away from the war – on trains packed with people and unable to take all those who are desperate to leave; or in cars passing through Russian checkpoints where anyone could be killed – as was the case for thousands of Ukrainian civilians trying to flee cities like Bucha, Irpin, Borodianka, and Mariupol.

There are stories of people who lost loved ones. Stories about those who will never respond to another message or hold those they cherish in their arms again. There are stories of becoming a widow while young, or of having to bury a child.

There are stories of Mariupol, where the dead were so numerous that they had to be buried in public squares and parks, or even in public courtyards. There are stories of Borodianka and Izium, in which apartment buildings were brutally bombarded by the Russians from the air, killing dozens and dozens of people.

There are stories of torture – of the Russians strangling prisoners, beating them, and using electroshocks.

This book is difficult to read. But it is nothing compared to what these people have gone through – and continue to go through. The pain you will feel is just a faint echo of the pain these people are feeling or have felt. We should read these stories to share this pain, at least a little bit; to know that evil has not disappeared, that it is here, that it is coming back regularly in history. Today one of its incarnations is Putinist Russia – a country that believes in violence and cruelty as fundamental principles.

Most of the Ukrainians we spoke to said they feel disgust and hatred towards the Russian occupiers. But they also felt confusion. This war is cruel – but also senseless. Its cruelty stems from its absurdity. The loss of sense and the loss of empathy go together. When people become blind and void of meaning, they also become indifferent to the sufferings of others, up to the point that they want to cause that suffering.

One of the roots of the Russian war against Ukraine is geopolitical. Russia wants to restore its empire which it fears losing forever. It is trying to make the 21st century into a century of re-imperialization, not de-imperialization. Whether Russia succeeds in this will depend on all of us.

However, another root is psychological. It is linked to the Russian attitude towards happiness and violence. There is something in the current Russian mentality that says: my only joy is the suffering of others. I will be happy only when others feel worse than me. I suffer but I will feel good if others suffer more than me.

This explains the macabre logic of this war: yes, Russians say, we will suffer, but Ukrainians will suffer more than us. This is the logic of their negative-sum game: I will lose in this war, but you will lose more than me.

This book is a testimony to all of this. It is evidence of cruelty. These stories are horrible to imagine. They would be difficult to read as fiction. But they are *non*-fiction.

I thank all the people who agreed to speak to us and publish their stories. I thank my colleague Olha Tatokhina, who listened to these stories and turned them into a text to read. I thank another colleague of mine, Alona Hryshko, for turning the idea for this book into a reality. I thank my colleagues from Dukh I Litera for publishing this book. I thank our wonderful team at UkraineWorld for running one of the most visible multilingual websites about Ukraine.

I thank Serhiy Zakharov, the talented Ukrainian painter who crafted the illustrations for this book, and who himself endured Russian torture chambers back in 2014 for daring to publicly support his country during the Russian occupation of parts of Donetsk of Luhansk regions in Eastern Ukraine. His drawings are rooted in his own experience of being tortured by people who care nothing for human dignity.

Ukraine needs peace, but it needs a peace that is just. A peace in which crimes are punished instead of rewarded. In which invasion are no longer options rather than a first choice. In which dictators lose rather than win. In which democracies are strong enough to protect themselves.

We are still a long way away from this world, but we hope it will one day be born. We must do whatever we can to help it emerge and become stronger.

Volodymyr Yermolenko,
Ukrainian philosopher and writer,
chief editor of UkraineWorld.org

Defending and Healing: Stories of Soldiers and Paramedics

"I meet my friends in cemeteries." 20-year-old writer Oksana became a soldier to defend her motherland

Oksana Rubaniak, call sign Xena, is a 20-year-old Ukrainian writer and soldier.

Now she serves as a machine gunner with the Black Zaporizhzhians 72nd Mechanized Brigade. Before the war, Oksana studied at university, worked in the Ivano-Frankivsk Department of Youth Policy and Sports, and co-founded a private school.

Oksana decided to join the Armed Forces of Ukraine on the first day of the full-scale Russian invasion. At first, she served in humanitarian missions in combat zones, but later took up arms herself.

After receiving a shrapnel injury near Vuhledar, Oksana Rubaniak was forced to return home to Ivano-Frankivsk to undergo treatment and rehabilitation. Although she is now safe, Oksana never stops worrying about her comrades and plans to return to the front.

> "One day, I will have a black ribbon on my photo. It's a matter of time. When you're on the frontline, your day of death approaches thousands of times," Oksana reflects.

"Many of my friends are gone. And where are your friends? They are walking, studying, and working. Mine were killed in battle with the enemy, while others are still fighting for their right to live every day. My fallen friends and I meet not in cafes, parks, or restaurants, but in the cemeteries. Conversations turn into hour-long monologues, watching our photos and videos together, and rarely appearing in our dreams.

I'm used to hearing it lately: "The soldiers will come back and make things right!" Are you sure they will come back? How many? Do you know how many Ukrainian soldiers have actually died during the Russian-Ukrainian war? Yes, we rejoice over the 200,000 mark of dead occupiers. But are you ready for the real number of posthumous Heroes of Ukraine? Are you ready to hear that most of the missing are dead, that their families' searches are pointless, and that their hopes are in vain?

Do you accept the fact that those who will return after the victory will want peace and quiet? They have been fighting all this time, and are exhausted and disappointed. They've lost their health, some have lost limbs, and almost all of them have contusions and psychological problems.

The military in the rear will face disrespect, injustice, and disorder. We will need to learn to coexist, not to blame, not to insult each other, but to coexist."

While she is away from the front, Oksana Rubaniak feels a kind of gap between civilians and the military in how people think. But despite being ready to die, Oksana still wants to live. After Ukraine's victory, she dreams of returning to her pre-war work of developing the private school she co-founded, along with writing poetry and prose.

"I have to be unbreakable." 19-year-old defender Ruslana lost her leg to Russian shelling

Ruslana Danilkina volunteered to defend Ukraine when she was 18 years old. During her first three weeks of service, she worked on "judicial investigations." Ruslana sometimes had to go to the frontline to get information.

After several of these trips, she realized that working with paper was not for her. She wanted to make herself useful in places where fighting was happening. Even though her commander did not want to take such a fragile young woman into his unit, Ruslana insisted.

Ruslana's relatives were not happy about her decision and were very worried for her. However, they accepted her choice and told her that she had to make her own choices for her own life.

Upon arriving at the front, Ruslana immediately began training as a communications operator, receiving and transmitting information about incoming munitions, the movement of equipment, infantry, and aviation, and any sounds and explosions. Ruslana also helped receive the wounded and dead and handed them over to medics.

"My work schedule was 24/7. An operator works day and night. It may seem like you're sitting in one place and just taking notes, but this is serious work. You have to be very alert and attentive, because something could happen at any moment, and you have to immediately report it to the higher command," said Ruslana.

Ruslana recalls that she felt incredible joy when she reported the enemy's coordinates to other units. She could hear outgoing Ukrainian rounds over her radio. "My heart rejoiced that we could avenge our people at least a little," she said.

On February 10, 2023, an air alert was announced throughout Ukraine. Ruslana and her comrades were on their way out for a combat mission. As she was answering a phone call from her brother, a shell hit their car.

In a state of shock, Ruslana recorded a video for her brother. She was sure that this would be her last video. Her leg had been torn off.

After being hit, time passed second by second. Ruslana was lucky to be picked up quickly and delivered to a hospital. The surgeon who treated her said that if she had been brought 10 seconds later, she would not have survived.

In the first two days after her injury, Ruslana did not want to live. "I was afraid that the world would not accept me, that I would be looked upon as a cripple, and that no one would have any use for me. I didn't know what to do and how I could overcome it," she recalls. She also felt unbearable pain. Ruslana's brother Vlad, his wife Anhelina, and her 4-month-old niece Olivia helped her to believe in herself again. Vlad promised his sister that she would get back on her feet and be able to live a full life. Within a day, he and his wife had scoured the internet for information about amputation, rehabilitation, and prosthetics.

> *"I decided that I should live for them. I was certain that I would one day walk and run with my little niece. I realized that I had to fight no matter what. To be unbreakable, like all our Ukrainians. Now I want to be a motivation for other people wounded and affected by the war so that they don't lose faith in life. I want to show by my example that it is possible to live a full life. The world should know and be able to accept such people," Ruslana says.*

Ruslana is currently in a hospital in Odesa and is continuing her rehabilitation. Her relatives are raising money for a modern, high-quality prosthetic. She dreams of returning to the Ukrainian Armed Forces as soon as possible.

He will never meet his friends again. Ukrainian soldier Ihor survived the enemy fire but lost his comrades

Before the full-scale Russian invasion, Ihor Hannenko was the director of a youth center. He traveled the world with his wife and was even a deputy on the Sumy Oblast Council. But everything changed on February 24, 2022, and Ihor took up arms to defend his country.

In his free time, Ihor has kept a blog in which he records the events that have happened to him during this war. We are publishing Ihor's story about being hit by a mortar in his voice.

***

An explosion. I open my eyes and I cannot understand what is happening. Launch, 2 seconds, hit. The enemy decided to scare us with mortars.

The third explosion, and only now do Kapral and I realize that we were sleeping without our body armor and helmets, which are near our shallow "pit." We had let our guard down, like idiots.

— "Now, once the shell lands, I'll quickly jump out and pull the bulletproof vests here, you will help me get 'em on," says Kapral.

— "OK."

Another shell falls closer. Usain Bolt himself would have envied the speed with which Kapral grabbed the bulletproof vests and got back down. We quickly get them on and try to stay as low as possible into the ground. The deeper you are in the ground, the better your chances to survive. It was good that the day before we had decided to deepen our trench by 10 centimeters. It was bad that it was not by 20-30.

A few shells fall even closer, and we realize that it was not just fire to spook us.

Russian mortars were adjusting their fire, which meant that an enemy drone with a thermal imager was flying somewhere above us. And this meant that we could only hope that the enemy would run out of ammunition before they hit us.

In such moments, your brain does not want to think at all. In movies, we see it as the main characters having their lives, loved ones, and other things flash before their eyes. That's all nonsense – the brain is just empty, an information vacuum. You just squeeze your legs together so that when the shrapnel hits, it doesn't immediately cut your artery, and you have a chance to apply a tourniquet and not bleed out.

A few more hits, and silence ensues.

— "It's finally over," I say.

— "Wait, it's a trap," replies Kapral, who already had combat experience in 2015-16. I have no reason not to believe him, so I continue to hold myself against the ground.

***

— "Who has a walkie-talkie, guys?" – we hear the cry of our friend Vedmid (Bear) from afar.

— "We don't have one, we don't know," we shout.

— "We need to ask for artillery support, otherwise we will all be killed here," shouts Vedmid, "The walkie-talkie is probably with the commander, I'll be back soon."

— "Don't go, the drone is adjusting. They'll see your movement and hit again."

***

But he could not hear us anymore. Here we heard the shell launch again and hit the ground. As Kapral said, it was a trap for inexperienced soldiers. I hope that Vedmid has managed to lie down in some hole.

A few more shells fall very close to us, and we hear screams that are more like the roar of a wounded animal. A person simply cannot shout like that.

— "I'm injured. AAAAH! Help!" – we recognize Vedmid's voice somewhere behind us.

— "Where are you wounded?" Kapral tries to shout to him.

— "Leg! LEEEEEG!" we hear Mishka's (that was his name) inhuman scream.

— "Put a tourniquet on!"

— "I can't, my hand!"

We understand that Vedmid has been badly cut by shrapnel, and no one but us can help him.

We do not see him, but only hear his screams and understand that he is lying 15 meters from us. Dragging a wounded man during shelling is not the best idea, but we impulsively decided that we had to do it anyway.

— "We will drag him between the hits," Kapral said.

— "They just fired. Now!" I answered, considering that we have a few seconds between launch and landing.

We jump up and rush to the wounded Vedmid. We feel the straps of his body armor and begin to pull him toward our trench. He weighs about 110 kilograms, if not more. He tries to grab my arm, but he cannot do it, because both his arms are riddled with shrapnel and are hanging only by a thread of muscle and tendon. He continues to scream in pain and because we are dragging him very roughly through the bushes, but there is simply no other way.

We hear another launch from the mortar barrel and immediately find ourselves in our trench, while Vedmid remains lying in the bushes.

— "You bastards," was all Kapral said before we jumped out again to drag our wounded comrade into our trench.

***

Only on the third time do we manage to move Mishka to our position. A few more shells fall, but we don't care about them anymore, because we have started examining his wounds.

"Yeah, an arm and a leg," I think, and I try to find his first-aid kit, "Where's your first-aid kit, where's the first-aid kit?," I'm about to scream. But I only hear the same inhuman shriek.

OK, the first aid kit must be on his vest, and at least one tourniquet must be on the body armor. I find it and put it on his leg. Immediately I feel a thick, warm liquid on my hands. Damn it, at all the training they said that you have to wear gloves, but to hell with gloves if it's just a couple of minutes more until he just bleeds out. Okay, I hope he doesn't have any deadly diseases.

***

Ihor and his comrade Kapral put tourniquets on both Vedmid's arms and made sure that his lungs were intact. Then they turned him over and realized that he had his scapula sticking out of his back. Just a living bone without muscles or skin. Without urgent evacuation, Vedmid had little chance of surviving.

When Ihor began to shout to call an evacuation vehicle, he heard the scream of another wounded soldier. It was Dania, and he had a bleeding leg. Ihor stopped his bleeding, after which Dania and Vedmid were dragged into a car that had just arrived.

That night, three of Ihor's comrades were seriously wounded and two, including the commander, died. It was an extremely hard moment for him.

"We would never see sunrises or sunsets together again. We stood around the dead and for a few seconds, everyone seemed to be saying goodbye. Everyone understood – we would never meet again. Not until another world. Watching this, I felt completely sick. I felt sorry for the guys. I couldn't hold back my emotions anymore, and the lump in my throat only got bigger. Without a word, I took a couple of steps away and turned away from the guys, and tears rolled down my cheeks…"

No happy birthday wishes. Ukrainian soldier Serhii spends his birthday in the trenches

The day before the full-scale Russian invasion, Serhii Yanchenko came to the Sumy territorial defense and left his information so that in the event of war, he could be quickly found and called to defend the city.

The start of the full-scale war on February 24, 2022 came as no surprise to Serhii. He was ready to protect the city and fight the Russian invaders. He received a weapon, and thus began his life as a soldier.

Serhii is now fighting in eastern Ukraine and occasionally publishes stories about his military experience on his Instagram.

We are publishing one of Serhii Yanchenko's texts in his voice.

***

June 16, 2022, 05:30 am. I have my birthday today, but there will be no happy birthday wishes. First, not everyone in the platoon knows about it, and second, we have been "at zero" [right on the front line – ed.] for more than a week. There has been no mobile connection. It is jammed by Russian electronic warfare measures.

I know that many people want to call and wish me a happy birthday today, but they will hear the phrase "that the subscriber is now out of reach." The hardest thing is now for my parents. They, more than anyone, want to talk to me. I imagine how many times my mom pressed on the green phone button near my contact in her phone.

I thought: well, what kind of gift can I make for myself? The answer was obvious. I turned on my phone, took my headphones, and turned on my musical playlist. What could be better than just listening to your favorite songs at five in the morning?

In the afternoon, the commander came to us. We warmed up the last drinking water reserves, brewing coffee and tea. There was very little water. One cup for two or three soldiers. I gave a stingy toast to my comrades. To the fact that I had the honor of defending our country with them.

"We have a gift for you, Siryi," said Kapral. "Take the drone and adjust the artillery fire on the enemy's positions. We've found a house where they often go."

I like gifts like that.

In the evening, we received the order to depart. Finally. We were tired, both physically and morally. We had lost guys here. They died right before our eyes. Some were seriously injured and have already been evacuated. But despite all this, we obeyed the order. We did not give up positions. But it was still necessary to go. And it won't be a stroll.

At night, we got on a bus, crossed it with all the prayers that we knew, and left. With all of us inside, it was packed like a train somewhere in Pakistan. Only one door worked – the rear.

"Siryi, your things have burned, I forgot to tell you."

"What? What does it mean – burned?"

"Well, your guys' backpacks were loaded into the Kamaz truck. There was still a place, and ammunition was put in the car too. I think grenade launchers were also there. There was a shelling at the power station. The shell hit the Kamaz, the ammunition was detonated, and the car was completely burned.

"Damn!" That's all I could say.

All the things I went to war with were burned. Three backpacks of all the essential stuff turned into ashes. I had trousers, a shirt, and army boots. And, of course, a machine gun.

The next morning we were in another city of Donbas, in our controlled territory. At that time, we did not know that the guys from the other brigade that replaced us would be stuck in our own positions in a couple of days. And we would see them in the military hospital in Dnipro.

We did not know that after a month and a half, the power station we had fought for would be taken by the enemy. This would be done by Wagner Group mercenaries – one of the enemy's most capable units.

***

After that, Serhii would lose many more comrades, but despite everything, he would continue to fight the enemy.

"I'll be here and do my best." Soldiers keep fighting through crushing fatigue

30-year-old soldier Khrystyna, call sign Kudriava (Curly), has served in the Armed Forces for 10 years. She studied at the Kharkiv National Guard Academy and later underwent international military training. At the start of the full-scale Russian invasion, Khrystyna was at a combat posting in Luhansk Oblast.

Since then, as the deputy commander of a mortar battery, she has been defending Ukraine in hot spots like Rubizhne, Sievierodonetsk, Lysychansk, and Bakhmut. The most difficult thing for Kudriava in this war has been the loss of her people.

Despite her inner strength and endurance, Khrystyna admits that she sometimes gets exhausted. This is what she has to say:

"I'm tired, too. I don't admit it, but it's true. I'm tired of living in the moment, just here and now, because that's all I have. Tired of reminding others that there is a war going on.

I'm tired of twitching whenever someone says out loud the numbers "300" (code for wounded) and "200" (code for killed in action), because these are not just mere numbers anymore. Tired of thinking about my guys in captivity and remembering those whom I'll never see again. Tired of thinking that one day I may not see those who are with me now.

I'm tired of not reacting to explosions, tired of distinguishing between a launch and a hit. Tired of not washing and not paying attention to my health. Tired of answering the question "How are you?" I'm very tired...

I'm tired of not wearing a dress and not allowing myself to be lighthearted. I'm tired of not crying. I'm even getting tired of all these words about fatigue.

But you know what? All, absolutely all fatigue, weakness, despair, pain, and everything else is unimportant. I'll be here and do my best. Because this is our way."

When Khrystyna thinks about the fact that people have the opportunity to rest in relatively safe regions of Ukraine, she is happy. It means that she and her comrades are doing a good job.

She knows that the most important thing is to believe in Ukraine's victory, to not lose heart, and to do everything she can to bring victory closer.

This soldier lost his arms and a leg during the war.
Zakhar was seriously injured and is now undergoing treatment abroad

Zakhar Biriukov joined the defense of Ukraine in 2015 because he did not want his country to be taken over by the Russians. Zakhar could not accept that Russians had started killing his countrymen and seizing towns and villages, so he chose to fight them.

As a soldier, Zakhar realized that a full-scale war was inevitable. He and his comrades did not know when exactly Russia would attempt a full invasion of Ukraine, but he was ready for it.

On February 24, 2022, Zakhar was visiting his parents in Zhytomyr Oblast, but when he learned that the war had started, he immediately went home to Vasylivka, Zaporizhzhia Oblast, where his wife and children were.

During the first month, Zakhar and his family remained in Vasylivka, which is now occupied by the Russian invaders. At that time, the town was in the gray zone, controlled by neither Ukraine nor the occupiers.

When the Russians began to intensify their shelling of Vasylivka, Yuliia and her children managed to leave the town and evacuate abroad. A week later, Zakhar also left for Zaporizhzhia. He was lucky to leave in time because the occupiers would certainly have come to capture or kill him.

On July 17, 2022, Zakhar was seriously injured by enemy fire. Doctors had to amputate his arms and right leg. He also sustained numerous burns, contusions, a broken jaw, eye damage, and serious blood loss.

In the first days after Zakhar's injury, doctors could not give any prognosis. His family was terrified and shed many tears. However, the main thing was that he was alive. His wife Yuliia, who was abroad with their children, returned to Ukraine and came to the hospital where Zakhar was being treated.

In the two months after his injury, Zakhar was in seven different hospitals.

"We all experienced a constant swing: his condition was critical, he could not be transported, and a few hours later he was already

in another city; in one hospital his leg was saved, and in another hospital, we were told that it had already been amputated because the bone had completely burned out; then there was positive news with his eye, and later we were informed that he needed to have it removed. And so on every day for two months," said Zakhar's sister Olesia.

After medical procedures in Ukraine, Zakhar and his wife went to Germany. He is now continuing his recovery at the University Hospital of Würzburg. The German doctors noted that their Ukrainian colleagues had done a very good job of fixing Zakhar's jaw and performing skin grafting. At first, Zakhar only stayed in the hospital, but after a few weeks, he moved to a dormitory near the rehabilitation center. During his stay in Germany, Zakhar has gained strength, has been visiting all the specialists he needs, and has been learning to use his body on his own.

Zakhar already has his first training prosthesis, with which he took his first steps after his injury. Zakhar will wear several types of training prostheses for six months, after which he will choose the most comfortable one.

Despite the pain and long-term complications of his treatment, Zakhar remains optimistic as he waits for his next surgeries and dreams of returning to Ukraine.

Living without both legs. Oleksii is a veterinarian who joined the army and was seriously injured in the war

Before the full-scale Russian invasion, 41-year-old Oleksii Prytula from Izmail, Odesa Oblast, worked as a veterinarian. After February 24, 2022, he prepared food for Ukrainian soldiers with his wife, helped IDPs, made camouflage nets, and donated blood.

Later, Oleksii joined the Ukrainian Armed Forces and took part in the counteroffensive to liberate parts of Kharkiv and Donetsk Oblasts from Russian occupation. On September 30, 2022, as he was evacuating a wounded comrade from the battlefield, he was wounded by enemy shell. His injuries forced doctors to amputate both his legs, and now he needs long-term rehabilitation and prosthetics.

In the first days of the war, Oleksii was turned away by the enlistment office because he had no military experience. At that time, it was mostly those who had fought before who were being recruited to defend the country from the invaders. However, on July 4, he received a call from the enlistment office and was informed that he had to be ready to go the next day.

Oleksii did not hesitate and quickly packed his things. His wife Yuliia, despite being worried for her husband and crying that night, accepted his decision.

Over the course of a month, he and other mobilized men learned to be soldiers. At the beginning of August 2022, Oleksii joined the 25th Airborne Assault Brigade. Oleksii spent his first week at the front near Bakhmut, monitoring the enemy's approach while under constant fire.

Because he had only been trained for war for a month, Oleksii was not prepared for the savageness of the bombardment.

> "The enemy was using their whole range of weapons on us: mortars, tanks, artillery, Grads, and aircraft. But we carried out our mission," he said.

Later, Oleksii and his comrades were transferred to the Kharkiv front. It was his brigade that liberated Izium from Russian occupation. During the assault, Oleksii even managed to take an enemy prisoner. He turned out to be a mobilized man from the so-called "Luhansk People's

Republic" who had been conscripted right in the middle of the street about a week before. The prisoner was even happy to be captured.

After Izium was taken and Ukrainian military control was established, Oleksii was assigned to work as a medic at an evacuation post near Lyman, Donetsk Oblast. His mission was to evacuate the wounded and dead from positions right on the front line.

Compared to Izium, where the Russians were simply fleeing, the enemy in Donetsk Oblast was fighting fiercely and furiously shelling Ukrainian positions. There were many casualties almost every day, so Oleksii had a lot of work to do.

This continued until the end of September when Oleksii himself came under enemy shelling. On September 30, while he was en route to evacuation points, the Russians launched Grad rockets at the vehicle carrying Oleksii, a driver, and a wounded soldier. All three managed to survive, but a while later, after the car had broken down from the damage of the barrage, a shell fragment hit Oleksii directly in his legs.

In a state of shock, Oleksii put bandages on both his legs and started shouting for help. Luckily, he was transported to a field hospital in time to undergo preliminary surgery. Oleksii's wife Yuliia told their 7-year-old daughter about her father's serious injury soon afterward. Trying to focus on the fact that her father was alive, Yuliia told her daughter that he would not have both legs. The girl burst into tears. At first, she was angry at her father for going to war, then at her mother for letting him go. But in the end, she directed her anger at Russia and Putin.

Oleksii later underwent surgery at a hospital in Kharkiv and was then transferred to Kyiv, where his legs were amputated. He is now undergoing treatment and waiting for his wounds to finish healing, which is not happening as fast as his doctors would like. Oleksii receives tremendous support from his wife Yuliia, their daughter, their friends, the veterinary community, his clinic's clients, and everyone who cared about him and his family.

Oleksii and his wife are also considering various options for prosthetics and trying to keep their fighting spirit, no matter what happens. After learning to walk with prosthetics, Oleksii Prytula would like to return to his brigade. However, if he is unable to fight, he will go back to working as a veterinarian.

Volunteer doctors save the lives of the Ukrainian soldiers. A mobile hospital provides medical assistance at the frontline

The Pirogov First Volunteer Mobile Hospital (PFVMH) is a volunteer initiative helping wounded Ukrainian soldiers on the frontline. It began its work in 2014, after the start of Russian aggression in eastern Ukraine. With the start of Russia's full-scale invasion of Ukraine, the hospital's geographical scope expanded.

PFVMH President and co-founder Hennadii Druzenko told us that the hospital's volunteers are people with a high drive for service and self-realization. They expect the most of themselves and the world.

Unlike many other units, PFVMH volunteers are professional medics. 95% of the Hospital's volunteers work for free. The unit's leadership provides financial assistance only to those who have been unable to keep their main jobs because of their time at the front. Unfortunately, there are such cases.

> "Instead of a rigid hierarchy, we advocate coordination in our work, solidarity instead of subordination, and service instead of earning money. In a certain sense, we are the exact opposite of the Wagner Group," Druzenko argues.

During the full-scale war, the PFVMH has specialized in the prehospital stage of medical care. The Hospital's volunteers, located 3-5 kilometers from the battlefield, work side by side with military medics to stabilize the wounded so they can be brought to hospitals alive. In particular, the PFVMH staff provides emergency life support to critically wounded soldiers all the way to the hospital.

"We help everyone. A wounded soldier is no different from a wounded civilian. When you take off their uniforms, soldiers and civilians look exactly the same," Druzenko explains.

A year ago, when the Hospital's volunteers were working in Bakhmut, most of their patients were civilians who had been hit by Russian fire. There were almost no local doctors left in the town, so people came to the volunteers. Today, 99 percent of PFVMH patients are wounded and ill soldiers.

Between May 2022 and April 2023, PFVMH provided assistance to 17,604 people, Druzenko says. This does not include those people whose names and diagnoses were not possible to record. According to Druzenko's estimates, at least one out of every ten wounded Ukrainian soldiers had been taken care of by the Hospital's medics at some stage of their medical treatment.

On average, PFVMH medics save about 1500 people every month. However, in recent months (as of May 2023 – Ed.), the number of wounded has gone through the roof, ranging from 2,500 to 3,000 people a month. There Hospital has about 80 personnel, half of whom are medics, with the rest including support staff like drivers, security guards, cooks, a press officer, an administrator, and so on. "Unfortunately, the war is not a planned surgery, and the flow of wounded does not stop here," says Druzenko. "To prevent our medics from simply falling dead of exhaustion, we have set up a schedule where, after working for one day, our doctors rest the next day. Overall, it is a complex system that requires readiness to evacuate and treat the wounded round the clock."

The first main problem PFVMH faces in its work is funding. According to Druzenko, the Hospital needs about $100,000 a month to maintain its ambulances, fuel its vehicles, and buy medical supplies, food, and other essentials. They somehow keep finding the money, but the organization has no stable sources of funding.

The second big challenge for PFVMH is ensuring it has enough medics. Since the beginning of the full-scale invasion, many specialists have left Ukraine, while others joined the Armed Forces. In addition, some managers are not ready to let their employees go to the front while leaving their main jobs waiting for them.

Every month, the Hospital announces a call for medics for a one-month rotation at the front. To join the PFVMH, volunteers need to fill out a registration form on the organization's website. The Hospital's top needs are emergency doctors like anesthesiologists, traumatologists, surgeons, operating nurses, and paramedics.

Druzenko recalls two stories that have served as particular motivation for the organization's volunteers to work and believe in miracles.

In June 2022, four children were playing in a yard in Pryvillia, a small village near Lysychansk, when the spot was struck by Russian Grad rockets, killing two boys on the spot. The two surviving girls were brought by PFVMH medics to a Bakhmut hospital. The oldest girl died there. The younger was brought to the Mechnykov Hospital in Dnipro. Fortunately, the younger sister survived despite her extremely serious condition. The Dnipro doctors told the PFVMH team that they had performed a real miracle, as by all indications, she would not have been expected to survive. This served as recognition of the organization's worth from one of the best and most experienced Ukrainian medical facilities.

The second case was with a soldier in the Sloviansk area. During a very difficult evacuation, the soldier's heart stopped four times, but the Hospital's doctors managed to restart it each time. When the soldier finally came to, he mentioned that that day happened to be his birthday. As he was being taken away after being stabilized, someone even brought a small cake into the ambulance.

"No matter how hard it is for us, when you remember these things, you find the strength to keep going and crawl on," Druzenko concludes.

The Fragility of Life: Stories of Childbirth and Children Amidst War

Childhood under fire. Valentyna's family fled the horrors of war

The atmosphere before the full-scale invasion was getting more and more depressing each day. Valentyna thought that the war would begin on her birthday, February 23, but she managed to celebrate in a peaceful Kyiv.

"On the morning of February 24, we were awakened by a phone call. "It has begun." We got up quietly so as not to wake the children. We prepared food and water in the hallway. We started carrying the mats and blankets to the basement. It was scary. I kept thinking, "Is this really happening?"

> "We went outside and heard explosions. Then the sirens. We slept in the cellar. I was very cold, because I fed the baby all night, and slept practically with one eye open. You run into that basement and think, what if a bomb hits here, or if someone comes here, and what to tell them, and where to run," she says.

Valentyna started teaching her older son Lev that he needed to take care of his little sister if anything were to happen. Valentyna explained what to say if he got lost, what to do if he heard an explosion or gunfire, or if their building caught fire. She felt herself beginning to cry as she was writing these instructions.

They lived 10 minutes from Irpin and constantly heard explosions and analyzed whether "that one was far" or "that was a little closer," and whether it was a missile, plane, or something else whizzing above their heads.

She was sick with fear, but Valentyna couldn't not eat because she needed to breastfeed her baby. She tried to cheer others up, cook food, and play board games in the basement. Thinking of others always made things easier.

Valentyna and her family lived like this for 5 days. Then they left because the temperature was dipping below freezing, which made sleeping in a small, damp cellar dangerous. Valentyna's daughter developed a runny nose, and it would be very terrible to get sick at that time.

The family arrived in a quiet place and started treatment for the baby. Valentyna barely slept during these days because she was feeding her baby. During the day, she watched her children sleep. And when they were safe, her body gave up. Valentyna felt that she had no strength at all.

"Now enemy missiles are periodically flying over our heads, but not so close. I hope they are shot down by our glorious air defense," she says.

An 8-month-old child was born under shelling.
Kateryna, his mother, tells their story

On February 24, 2022, I was 7 months pregnant. I woke up at 5 am and went to the toilet. But I couldn't fall asleep because the neighbors from above were running and shouting. A woman ran out of the entrance with her child and ran somewhere.

It was strange, so I started reading the news. I was in shock: explosions in Kyiv, Kharkiv, and Vinnytsia. The war had started. Russia had attacked Ukraine, cruelly at night, while everyone was sleeping.

I woke up my husband, and we turned on the TV: everywhere was on fire. We began to think about what to do, and then we heard something flying. Not like a plane. Suddenly something exploded, and I thought the windows would fly out. I ran to my daughter's room to pick her up. She did not understand what was happening.

We quickly gathered our documents, clothes, food, and water. We decided to buy more groceries, so my husband went to the store. And there were already queues on the street. There was nowhere to withdraw money, and there were lines for kilometers at gas stations.

I was shaking, and so was my daughter. My husband bought what he could. We texted our parents, and we thought about ways to communicate in case mobile service was cut. We listened to the news all the time.

We stayed in Kyiv until March 4. During the first air raid sirens, we went to the basement, but it was so damp and cold that I couldn't stay there with my pregnancy. Before the war, I got sick with Covid, and in the basement I got sick again. We decided to stay at home.

We used to sit in the corridor during the air raid alarms, and at night we put our daughter to sleep there, because we couldn't fit together. We prayed that we would wake up in the morning. Our windows were boarded up. It was dark. We hardly spoke during the first days. We couldn't sleep.

> *I cried every day out of fear for my daughter, my unborn son, and my loved ones. Sometimes there were days of despair, and my husband calmed me down as best he could.*

We decided to go to a safer place. Eighteen hours on the road, sitting, without being able to rest, is not easy for a pregnant woman. But we arrived and for the first time since the beginning of the war, we were able to sleep peacefully.

We stayed in Ukraine, as I was not going to go abroad under any circumstances. I simply couldn't leave everyone I loved. For me it would be worse than living in fear of rocket attacks. So we lived in the village with relatives.

On March 14, we quietly celebrated our daughter's 10th birthday. We started to think about where to go to give birth. There was almost a month and a half left before the birth. We had to buy some things for it, because we took almost nothing from home.

But on the night of March 20, my water broke. I was in my 8th month. The ambulance took me first to one hospital, then they took me to another one which could handle a premature baby.

On March 21, as I was giving birth, when I couldn't get up and go anywhere, an air raid alert began. Doctors had to deliver in the hospital, not in the bomb shelter. And so at 4:10 pm my son Yaroslav was born.

We spent 2 weeks in the hospital. During air raid alarms, I grabbed my son, turned off all the sensors and drips, wrapped him up warmly, and we ran to the shelter. Sometimes we sat there for 5 hours, and we ran there many times each day. This is a great stress for premature babies. We heard explosions and missiles flying.

While I was in the hospital, terrible things were happening in Ukraine: the murder of civilians, violence against children, women, and men. It was a real genocide of the Ukrainian people.

We returned to Kyiv when Yaroslav was not yet a month old because a premature baby needs doctors, supervision, and medicine. All this was almost absent in the village where we were staying.

We are now living at home, close to family and friends. I think about the war every single day. I still cry sometimes, as the news still hurts. Our people are dying, and in some cities they are still sitting in basements. Our soldiers are dying. But we know what we are fighting for.

We're on our land. Ukraine will win.

Giving birth Day 1. Yuliia's son was born on February 24, 2022, in Kyiv

It was our long-awaited first pregnancy. Until the 8th month, I was working as a makeup artist. I loved my job and was preparing to meet my baby. The doctors gave me a due date of March 1.

On February 23, 2022, all the news was about the war. I couldn't believe it. Then I was more worried about my well-being, so I quickly fell asleep. My husband was nervous that night.

On the morning of February 24, we were in Kyiv, on the left bank of the Dnipro. My husband and I woke up at the same time to loud explosions. I looked at him with frightened eyes. He took his phone, read something and said that the war had begun. At that moment, panic and fear came over me.

I grabbed my stomach and went to the bathroom to breathe. At that moment, I was thinking only about my child. "You can't panic!" I told myself. But these words hardly had any effect. Then my husband said to quickly collect what we needed.

Where? Why? We got into our car and thought about what to do. The city had begun to panic, and there were queues at gas stations. It was risky to go to the West of Ukraine. At that time, I could have gone into labor at any minute. We stayed in Kyiv.

My husband decided to move to the right bank of Kyiv and stay in a hotel near the maternity hospital. We got there quickly, checked in, and had breakfast. I was very tired, so I immediately fell asleep in the room. An hour later, we were asked to move out, because there was a military base next to the hotel, which meant a high risk of missile strikes.

We went to another hotel. We got out of the car, and my first contraction began. I was breathing. "Probably false. But very painful," I thought. We settled in. The second contraction, and a third half an hour later.

We called the doctor and went to the maternity ward. I was glad that it did not happen on the road and we made the right decision to stay in Kyiv. We reached the hospital in 5 minutes.

> *An air raid alarm began, but the doctors continued delivering to the sound of the siren. I am very grateful for this, because many women had to give birth in bomb shelters.*

It all happened very fast. My son probably understood that the situation was urgent. 15 minutes after we were moved to the ward, the siren sounded again. The medical staff urged everyone down to the bomb shelter. Pregnant women and women who had just given birth were all sitting there. I was holding my baby tightly in my arms, wrapped in a blanket. It was cold. My husband was always by my side.

After 2 hours, we were allowed to go up to the ward and rest. After 20 minutes, we all ran to shelter again. All the mothers were overwhelmed with fear for their children. Tired, exhausted, some having just given birth, and some with contractions, they were all in the dark basement, sitting on wooden benches. Women who had difficult births lay on the floor moaning.

In the morning, we were discharged and sent home, because the maternity ward was overcrowded. New pregnant women were constantly arriving. The bomb shelter couldn't accommodate everyone, and no provisions were coming in at all.

We went to my mother outside the city. Every night we went down to the cellar. I breastfed my baby covered with a blanket in the freezing cold. This lasted for two weeks.

My husband couldn't stand it and decided that our son and I should go to the Czech Republic. I did not want to leave without my husband, but my maternal instincts kicked in. We went by car. My baby was two weeks old. It was a four-day journey. With 7-10 hour waits at the border.

We had to spend the night in the car at gas stations because all the hotels were full. Checkpoints, constant air alerts, curfew, 24/7 stress and fear. I held on, only praying for my child.

I was devastated inside and despaired in my soul. Exhausted, we reached the Czech Republic. There I fully realized what had happened and cried a lot. I was in denial and felt constant anxiety inside. But that's another story.

"Almost nothing is left of our city." Anna tells a story of Lysychansk, where she and her new baby were born

Anna did not expect the war at all. She says that everything in her city was quiet and peaceful, everyone was living their own life. She had an apartment which she was renovating, and she recently had a baby.

On the first day of the full-scale war, Anna heard a strange sound. Then, somewhere around 7 a.m., the whistling started. She saw something like red streaks in the sky.

In the neighborhood next to Anna's, the Russians struck a nine-story building. They hit it right in the middle. There were more explosions in the evening. There were no military facilities or bases there. Absolutely nothing. But every day, more planes flew overhead.

On the tenth day of the war, there was almost no living space left in the city. Shops were closed, the water supply was cut off, and there was no electricity or communications. People carried water from wells. Anna, for example, walked with her small child. She had no husband because the couple had broken up.

Later, the shelling became so intense that handles flew off of the plastic windows in Anna's apartment. One day, a shell hit a neighboring house. The explosion left a huge hole in the building. It was then that Anna decided to leave.

> "It was all so terrible. We have the Russian border nearby. All people lived peacefully and in harmony. Why did this war start? Why did this aggression from Russia appear when no one ever expected it? Almost nothing is left of our city," says Anna.

In Lysychansk, the Russians bombed residential buildings, schools, and shops. Anna saw the results with her own eyes: "Bodies were lying near houses on the streets, and the neighbors covered them with blankets and other things. Everything nearby was destroyed. The bus stop was crushed like a tin can. Imagine the force of the impact, which sent concrete slabs flying onto a nearby street, and shrapnel gutted houses and shattered windows."

After Anna and her daughter had already left Lysychansk, the Russians targeted the Donbas shopping center. There was a huge fire.

The Central Market burned for two days. Near the market, there were residential buildings and two schools. They were also affected by this explosion.

Anna's friend has a relative living in Russia. The Russians don't believe that their soldiers are firing at Ukrainians. They say that this was so-called "liberation."

Anna has a message for Russian soldiers:

"You also have children! Small or adult who went to war. Stop this horror. We are all people. Look at my daughter, look at your children. Are you not thinking about your own children when you are shooting? You wouldn't shoot at your child! Why are you shooting at our children, why are you shooting at us, why are you bombing us? We haven't done anything bad."

This text is based on testimony collected by the Kharkiv Human Rights Protection Group.

"I had one goal." Olena fled the war with two small children

In March 2022, 29-year-old Olena Pashynina was forced to leave Kharkiv with her two daughters: 5-year-old Lera and 4-month-old Sonya. Olena's husband Vladyslav serves in the Armed Forces.

Before the full-scale Russian invasion, the family lived happily: they had purchased and furnished a new house and had taken holidays. Lera was in kindergarten and participated in various hobby groups. The Pashynins also had a dog, which Olena unfortunately had to leave with good people in Poltava, as it would have been too difficult for her to go abroad with two children and a dog.

Olena and her husband had talked about the unfolding situation on February 23. Given that Vladyslav was serving in the military, he told Olena that the following day she would take their child to kindergarten alone because he would be moving to his barracks.

Olena resented this, as it took a lot of effort to take Lera and the baby together. At that time, Olena did not believe that the Russians would actually invade.

Olena tried to convince her husband that Putin's threats were nonsense, that Ukraine was panicking, that nothing like that would happen, and that, in the 21st century, everything could be solved with words. Vladyslav told her he hoped she was right but asked her to pack a suitcase all the same.

On the morning of February 24, 2022, Olena and her husband woke to the sound of explosions and a phone call. Vladyslav's father called and told them that the neighborhood of Saltivka was being bombed. Olena ran to wake up her older daughter and began to gather their things.

Vladyslav then received the call to report for duty. Olena remained at home alone with the children and, to ensure they wouldn't be afraid, Olena's mother-in-law and her sister came over too.

At first, the family did not go down to the basement; despite hearing rounds of Grad fire, they remained where they were. However, on the third day, they heard the sound of aircraft and things became much more frightening. That was when Olena and her relatives decided to hide in the basement, even though it was very cold and uncomfortable.

> "On the sixth day of the war, I realized that remaining at home was extremely dangerous and that my children and I might not wake up the next day. My husband stopped by the house for a moment because volunteers with the Territorial Defense unit were delivering diapers to everyone in need, and that included us. We were in the kitchen and I heard the wild cry, 'Get down!!!' That's how we learned what a "Sushka" was," Olena explains.

A "Sushka" is a Sukhoi jet fighter, and this one flew directly over Olena's house. Out of fear, the family ran and hid under the table. "It was such a hellish roar, such a crazy sound, that we hugged each other to the point where we bruised each other's arms. Then we got out and my husband explained what it was. We understood that the war would not be the same as before, that it had now acquired a different color," Olena said.

The next time Olena and her children were sheltering in the basement during heavy shelling, crying and shaking from the noise of the aircraft, she realized that she had to leave Kharkiv. Her mother-in-law did not support her idea at the time, as she believed that driving through the city under artillery fire would be suicide. Back then, there were ever-growing instances of people dying simply by trying to save themselves.

"I never considered myself a strong person, but I realized at that moment that I had one goal. I left the basement and started to seek acquaintances who could help. Fortunately, I have a very large social circle and there were many people who helped me get from Ukraine to Germany," Olena explains.

Olena and her daughters first traveled to Poltava, where they stayed with an acquaintance she had studied with at university. Dmytro, a volunteer who had helped Olena's husband in his Territorial Defense unit, helped with their evacuation. As she left Kharkiv, Olena witnessed the scale of the destruction and she felt overwhelmed with feelings of hatred and hopelessness. Instead of the usual two hours, the journey to Poltava took the family 15 hours.

In Poltava, Olena decided that, for the sake of her children's safety, she had to go abroad. Together with other families, they traveled for four days to reach the Hungarian border. From there, Olena and her daughters reached Munich, where her friend Olha was already waiting for them.

Olena spent two days in Munich, at Olha's house, and eventually settled in the city of Bad Tölz as guests of a German family of dentists, who run their own clinic.

Olena is sincerely grateful to the volunteers and kind people who helped her on her long journey abroad and who have provided her with everything she needs in Germany. She now attends sessions with a psychologist and dreams of returning to her home in Kharkiv. Olena's husband Vladyslav was wounded in the war and is currently undergoing treatment.

This text is based upon testimony collected by the Kharkiv Human Rights Protection Group.

With kids amidst missiles falling nearby. Yuliia evacuated her three children under a torrent of enemy missiles

In the first months of the war, Mariupol resident Yuliia Belei lived in a basement with her children, drinking rainwater and burying neighbors in the yard. Yuliia's husband is a soldier and is currently defending Ukraine from the Russian invaders.

Before the war, the Belei family lived well, with regular holidays and trips to the sea, the local zoo, and parks. Yuliia's eldest daughter was a fifth grade schoolgirl, while the two younger ones went to kindergarten. Yuliia worked as a store baker and loved her job.

From the first bombing in Mariupol on the night of February 24, 2022, Yuliia was unable to go to work. She is relieved that this happened at a time when she was with her children.

When Yuliia heard the sound of incoming projectiles, she knew it was somewhere nearby. She called her husband who was on duty and asked him what was going on. However, he did not want to worry her and he told her everything was under control and that she should go to bed.

Then Yuliia heard an explosion so loud that she was sure the windows in her apartment had been blown out. She thought it was shelling from truck-mounted Grad missiles but then realized it was coming from the air.

At 5 o'clock in the morning, Yuliia heard a new explosion and the news officially announced that the war had begun. "I don't understand why [the Russians] want this war; I don't understand what they want to prove by this, but they will not have Ukraine, or Mariupol either. Mariupol will always remain Ukrainian," Yuliia explains.

After that, Yuliia woke her eldest daughter and told her that the war had begun. Her husband called her and asked her to leave the city, telling her to take warm clothes and get out of the city.

Since Yuliia did not have a car, she did not know what to do or where to go. Not only that, but she had very little cash to pay for transportation. Yuliia decided to wait for things to quiet down outside, withdraw money from her bank card and think about what to do next.

After standing in a long queue for the ATM, she finally managed to withdraw some cash. On the way back home, Yuliia saw Ukrainian tanks, armored personnel carriers, Grad truck-mounted missiles, and a lot of infantry.

A neighbor then took Yuliia and her children to the center of Mariupol, where there was less shelling at that time. She tried to leave the city by car, but they were not allowed to pass through the checkpoint. Soldiers explained to her that there was a lot of firing from the air, and they could be killed on route.

Then Yuliia went to the Terrasport complex, where there was a shelter and where people could feel safe. It was very cold there and the people slept on large mattresses on the floor. The children were very scared because of the shelling and worried about their dad. Yuliia's youngest, her three-year-old daughter, did not understand what she was feeling yet, and six-year-old Ivanka was worried, constantly tugging at Yuliia and asking her to call her dad. Her oldest daughter kept herself together very well and did not panic.

The next day, Yuliia and her neighbor went home to collect their pets and some belongings. On the way, they saw many burnt cars and destroyed buildings. It was frightening to turn back with missiles falling nearby. The neighbor stepped hard on the gas and quickly turned the car around.

Yuliia and her children remained in the Terrasport shelter until March 1. The sports complex announced online that there were too many people there and there was simply nowhere to accommodate them all. The administration asked anyone who could to take people into their own homes.

Thus, on March 1, Yuliia and her daughters went to stay with complete strangers: Serhii and Oksana. The couple took their children to Malynivka, a village 20 km from Mariupol, and returned to help the Ukrainian army. Serhii and Oksana's apartment was located near Terrasport, on the first floor, from where they could quickly get down to the basement.

There was no heating in the apartment, but there was still electricity, water, and a telephone line. Yuliia and the children could still bathe and prepare food. At one point, Oksana offered to fill a tub with water just in case. Fightingwas already underway, and anything could happen.

On March 3, Yuliia was awoken by a loud explosion nearby. The power and water were cut off. Yuliia's family, Serhii, and Oksana took warm clothes and some food and went down to the basement. Other residents of the building also gathered there. On that day, enemy planes dropped many bombs, shaking everything, even in the basement.

Heavy bombing continued until March 7. Yuliia lost all contact with her relatives. On March 4, she tried to leave Mariupol with her children. Serhii and Oksana discovered that many Mariupol residents had organized a convoy to leave, so they decided to take advantage of this opportunity. They painted the word CHILDREN on the car and set off. Driving through the city, they saw many dead bodies of civilians. Some were covered up, but others were just lying there.

Shortly after their car had joined the column and started moving, missiles began to fall, some hitting the ground right in front of the cars. The cars had to dodge the explosions and craters, with missiles still falling.

> "We realized that the next missile could hit our car. Two cars in front of us had caught fire. They also had the word CHILDREN written on them. And the drivers were also women. There were children there ..." Yuliia recalls.

Serhii realized that it was dangerous to travel any further. He turned around and drove back. "The more we drove, the more missiles came falling behind us. It was frightening to look around and all I could do was cover the children as best I could. I told them to sit bent over so, God forbid, not a single shard would hit them," Yuliia said. People were burned alive in the cars driving in front of them. They were trapped where they were.

Yuliia finally returned to Serhii and Oksana's apartment and remained there for the next few days. They cooked food on the street with firewood, because the gas pipeline had been cut. However, Yuliia understood that she needed to get out of Mariupol as soon as possible. The explosions were getting louder, and the Russians were getting closer.

Then the water supply was cut. Fortunately, it was raining so the people collected the rainwater and drank it. Sometimes they boiled the water, while on other occasions they simply drank it as it fell, when there was no more tea. Yuliia and her neighbors broke off branches from the trees and brewed cherry tea.

Collecting cleaner water for the children meant walking 1–2 kilometers. Yuliia took the risk to fetch under gunfire and shelling. When shells flew nearby, she would fall to the ground, face down in the mud, next to dead bodies.

> "Buildings caught fire every day; three or four new ones each time. One apartment building with five entrances was destroyed by an aerial bomb and collapsed in the middle from top to bottom. People were living there at the time," Yuliia said.

Due to the constant shelling, there were too many bodies for the city to handle, so people were forced to bury the dead themselves. Yuliia and her neighbors buried two soldiers and two local residents who had died from shrapnel wounds.

Yuliia decided to leave Mariupol, despite all the risks, when she encountered theRussian soldiers stationed at a school near Serhii and Oksana's house. One of the occupiers told Yuliia that if she wanted to leave, she had until 4 pm that day. However, the only possible route was through the so-called DPR.

Although Yuliia's husband had warned her not to use the green corridor of the DPR under any circumstances, she decided she had no choice. She and her children would simply die in Mariupol.

In the end, Serhii took Yuliia and her daughters to Volodarske. There were Russian flags everywhere and Russian soldiers were walking around. Yuliia approached a volunteer and told her she wanted to go to Manhush. She replied that Rostov was now the only evacuation route available. Yuliia could not go to Russia. She did not want to in the first place, but as the wife of a Ukrainian soldier, she could have been imprisoned or even killed.

Yuliia still managed to find people who were evacuating to Ukraine. Despite the thorough inspections at Russian checkpoints, they were able to reach Berdiansk. From there, Yuliia and her children continued to Zaporizhzhia, and then to Lviv. Today her three children are living in Poland, and her husband continues to fight for a free, independent Ukraine.

This text is based on testimony collected by the Kharkiv Human Rights Protection Group.

"We will no longer have the life we had before."
Yevheniia evacuated with her daughter due to continuous Russian shelling

Before the full-scale Russian invasion, Yevheniia Savynska lived with her husband and daughter in the village of Kyinka in Chernihiv Oblast. Constant shelling forced the family to evacuate to Chernihiv, and then to Khmelnytskyi.

Yevheniia's husband is a soldier and, at the end of February 2022, his unit was stationed right where the family lived. On one of the first days of the invasion, the Russian occupiers unleashed a heavy bombardment on the village, killing 35 Ukrainian soldiers.

"When the debris was cleared after the shelling, one boy was found in five parts. I say 'boy' because we later found his cap and documents, detailing his name, surname, and year of birth – 1998. I remember that his name was Dmytro," Yevheniia said.

The dead also included a man who had retired a week before the invasion. When the war started, he said he wanted to fight and he asked for a weapon. He died 4 days later. He had already retired; he did not have to do this.

During the enemy attacks, Yevheniia and her daughter hid in the bomb shelter of a nearby house. The people there had prepared the shelter well: they had stocked up on provisions, brought things that they had taken with them from the village in the summer, and some gas cylinders. After the shelling, the gas, water, and power supplies in the village were all lost, so these preparations turned out to be most prudent.

> "We didn't sleep at all, of course. Everything was booming and shaking. There were a lot of people in the bomb shelter," Yevheniia recalls.

At one point, her 11-year-old daughter admitted that she thought she was going to die. Yevheniia asked her why she thought this, to which the girl replied, "I realized that there will be an apple tree, our mulberry tree, there will be sky, there will be sun, and I will be gone." These adult words shocked and frightened Yevheniia.

There were about thirty people hiding in the small, 20 square meter basement . There were also pet cats and dogs. It was a very difficult time, both physically and psychologically, as the bombing was so intense. Some time later, Yevheniia's husband took her and her daughter from Kyinka, along with several other people. Later, everyone was evacuated from the village.

Yevheniia moved from Kyinka to Chernihiv and lived with her husband's parents in the city center. It was also very loud there, with aircraft flying overhead constantly and multiple explosions. Yevheniia had felt needed in her village, where she had been helping the soldiers. Here, though, she did not know what to do. She got her friends and neighbors together and they decided to donate blood.

"We had just finished giving blood and had left the center. There were what must have been kilometer-long queues for food, which was very hard to find. Just then, an aircraft flew over Chornovol street, which was very close by. Everything within a 3 kilometer radius was damaged. The girls and I hid for about four or five hours, making short dashes from one bomb shelter to another, then another. Although it is only 20–25 minutes from there to my husband's parents, the journey took us four and a half hours. His parents, of course, had turned gray, already resigned to the fact we would not return," Yevheniia explains.

On March 17, Yevheniia and her daughter left for Khmelnytskyi. At that moment, there was no water or power anywhere in Chernihiv. There were also problems with food. Yevheniia's husband asked her to leave so that he could do his job and not worry about them.

Several days later, they arrived in Khmelnytskyi. Yevheniia woke up at night because her daughter was crying. She said, "Mom, why didn't I value my life? Why didn't I appreciate my school, my friends? My hobby groups?"

The girl studied singing, Italian, and art. Her drawings have been displayed at various exhibitions. Then she said, "Why didn't I appreciate it? We will no longer have the kind of life we had before the war." It was these words that left the most lasting impression on Yevheniia. Not the bombs, but the fact that her child had suffered such moral damage.

This text is based on testimony collected by the Kharkiv Human Rights Protection Group.

Saving her daughter from a city under fire. The story of Svitlana from Kharkiv

Before the war, Svitlana Borodina lived in Kharkiv and worked as a designer in an advertising agency.

A few weeks before the full-scale Russian invasion, Svitlana and her friends began considering the possibility of war. The teachers at her 16-year-old daughter's school also raised the matter and told her to prepare for it.

On the evening of February 23, 2022 Svitlana's daughter asked to sleep with her, because she was feeling anxious. At 5 am on February 24, 2022, Svitlana woke up to strange sounds. At first, she thought that there must have been a special occasion and that people were setting off fireworks. However, 5 am was not a normal time to be doing this.

> "I went out onto the balcony and realized the noise was not stopping. I was living almost in the center of the city, so I couldn't see where the noise was coming from. People who lived in the areas where the shelling began saw everything straight away. There were blasts and a glow in the sky. I messaged an acquaintance on Facebook and asked what was going on. The answer confirmed my worst fears and I woke my child and told her that, "Sweetheart, the war has started," Svitlana recalls.

Svitlana later read in the news that explosions had been heard in Kyiv, Chernihiv, Lviv, Odesa, and Dnipro. She and her daughter packed their things, then spent the next 4 days alone at home, in the bathroom, where they made a bed. They even spent the nights there.

It was terrifying when a fighter jet flew past Svitlana's house for the first time. After that, she and her daughter went down to the basement and remained there for six days and nights.

When a Russian missile struck the building of the Court of Appeals, which is located 300 meters from Svitlana's house, she realized that it would not end soon and that she had to leave Kharkiv.

Svitlana wanted to take her elderly parents with her, but they flatly refused to evacuate. Her mother told her, "Pack your belongings and go; we'll figure things out here ourselves. You need to get your child out." Svitlana put on a brave face and began preparations to leave.

At first, Svitlana tried desperately to call a taxi, but no one would take her call. It took about 45 minutes to walk to the station, but it was a frightening experience, with constant shooting and explosions all around. In the end, Svitlana's friends helped her find a car to pick them up and transport them to the station.

There were a lot of people at the station. Svitlana had never seen such a crowd in Kharkiv, even during the Maidan events. She told her daughter that they would take the first train to arrive. As a result, they first took one train to Vinnytsia, and from there they took another to Lviv. Since Lviv was already overcrowded at that time, Svitlana and her daughter were accepted in Drohobych, which is where they still reside.

Svitlana's parents live in Kharkiv thanks to the help of volunteers and a number of organizations. Svitlana purchased some medicines in Drohobych that were not initially available in the city and she mailed them to her parents.

When Svitlana was still in Kharkiv, she saw a rocket hitting the Nikolskyi mall. There was a lot of smoke and she was terrified. She also said that the Russians had intended to capture the city; they broke through the defensive lines at certain places and advanced in tanks, armored personnel carriers, and other combat vehicles.

First, the locals heard automatic gunfire, followed by louder sounds. The Kharkiv territorial defenses engaged the invaders and a battle began. Russian soldiers occupied School No. 134. They were eventually defeated, but the school was destroyed and cannot be restored. While the loss of the school's historic building is lamentable, the Russians were stopped and were unable to capture Kharkiv.

Many of Svitlana's friends and acquaintances from Kharkiv and its surroundings have had their houses damaged or completely destroyed. She says that Kharkiv residents now simply hate Russians: "I think they would tear them to pieces if they were given the opportunity."

This text is based on testimony collected by the Kharkiv Human Rights Protection Group.

In the Clutches of Grief: Stories of the Loss of Loved Ones

Tears of a Soldier's Widow. A letter from a wife left behind

Now I will write the most frightening words of my life. I cannot write, I want the whole world to scream what you were like. And without you, I can only do one thing – write.

I'm sitting next to my dead husband. My life lies next to me in a closed coffin. My life wiped my tears and said that it would never leave. Who stroked me all night when I was sick. It's like I don't exist anymore.

You were the best in everything. Not because you are mine. That's just how it was. You were never afraid of anything. You smiled every day, even if everything was bad. "I am warmly dressed and ate well" – that was your attitude for all occasions.

And you always helped me. I could ask for anything. "Are you a commander?" you joked with a sly smile. "Worse," I said, "I'm the commander's wife," and kissed you on the nose. I could tell you things that I would never tell anyone, and you always understood.

I knew how unbearable we would have been in old age, I knew what kind of eyes our children would have. I've been thinking about what to get you for our first wedding anniversary. And I had to choose a wreath for your grave.

You are an officer with such an internal code of honor that these bastards could not even dream of. You are my heart! You are my soul! I love you to infinity and am proud of you. I curse these fascists for you, for our unborn children, for the stolen life, yours and mine.

I'm sitting next to my dead husband. I am a widow at 25. These inhumans stole my life. F*cking Russia stole my life.

Shattered Dreams and Meaning of Life. The story of Maryna Baliaba from Bucha, whose husband died in the war

At 6 am, Maryna's father-in-law called her and said that the war had begun and that they should stay at home instead of taking her son to kindergarten. She thought, "What is he talking about? This cannot be!"

"How naive I was. I got up and opened the window. The chill immediately hit me in the face. But there were other sounds that had never been here before. I had heard something similar when I went to my husband for a rotation in Mariupol in 2015. Was it shelling?"

"But stop, I'm not in Mariupol, I'm in BUCHA! This is 2022! In the suburbs of Kyiv! What shelling? It was a shock. I didn't believe it. I called my husband and cried. He said to pack up and stay with our son at all times. For the first time in my life, I felt a wild, animalistic fear," Maryna said.

There was no mobile connection. They went to the grocery store and waited in line for 2.5 hours. At noon Russians started bombing the Hostomel airport. It is not far from their house. Planes, helicopters and rockets flew over them. It was like a Hollywood action movie, but in real life.

The fighting began, which turned into occupation. There was constant shelling. There was no electricity, no gas, no water, and no communication. Maryna lived like this with her son for 24 days until Russian soldiers came to their house.

They searched the house and walked with their dirty boots on Maryna's floors, which she and her husband had spent so long picking out. Russians set up quarters in neighboring houses. Maryna's family understood that Ukrainian troops would force Russians out during their counteroffensive and that she and her son were now in even greater danger.

The next day they left in an evacuation column to Kyiv, and then to the center of Ukraine. She was broken. But an even more terrible blow awaited Maryna. Her husband was killed on March 30. It was her birthday. "Life has stopped. I died with him," she added. "We planned to give birth to a baby girl. Kylyna or Melanka. To have a church wedding. To go to the sea. Insulate the house. Make repairs. Buy a car. But now I have to do it myself," Maryna says.

"Russia has taken away from me the most important thing – the meaning of life. I don't know how to live anymore. And is it necessary?"

"I want to take your hand and not let it go." Alla's boyfriend was killed by a Russian shell

Alla Karpenko was in a relationship with paratrooper Yevhenii Bazylevskyi, who fought near Bakhmut, Donetsk Oblast. During the full-scale Russian invasion, Yevhenii served in the 46th Separate Airborne Brigade. He had served in hot spots in Ukraine since 2015.

On December 17, he was killed by a Russian shell at 27 years old. After the death of her beloved, Alla began keeping a public diary on her social media.

"The shrapnel flew right into your head, pierced your lung, and shattered your leg. As you said, bullets don't like you. But shrapnel and mines are following you. I won't believe in your death until I see it with my own eyes. As I go to take your body, there is still a lingering hope that there is some misunderstanding. That you in fact survived. No matter what Yehorka (the company commander) saw, he could be wrong," Alla wrote on the way to Dnipro, where Yevhenii's body was taken.

"I want to see you, take your hand and not let it go for a long time. To kiss your fingers, as you always kissed me. To hug the chest in which the heart beat so rhythmically when I hugged you for the last time. I have never cried in front of you. Sorry, I'm going to break my promise. But I still hope you're alive."

Alla spoke to Yevhenii for the last time on December 13. Then they could not contact each other because he was on a combat mission. On December 17, he was killed in the line of duty.

"On December 13, I wrote to you that I really wanted to hug you. You said you did, too, but you had to take a shower first. In war, there are no showers, only wet wipes. You didn't see that message, but I wrote that I loved you even smelly and unwashed. That's how I'll see you today: bloody, dirty and mutilated. But I love you anyway," Alla wrote on Facebook. Alla understood that her beloved had indeed been killed when she came to the morgue. A bodyguard held her in one hand so that she wouldn't faint, while with the other she stroked Yevhenii's cold body. "You're as handsome as always. Your head seems to be intact. But there are a lot of holes in your chest."

Alla wanted to hold Yevhenii's hand during the entire journey from

Dnipro to Kyiv, but it was impossible because his body had to be kept refrigerated.

> *"I haven't cried since yesterday. I no longer have the strength for this. It's just a pity that St. Nicholas will give some sweets and gifts under the pillow to good girls, and I will get your death certificate."*

The last time Yevhenii visited Alla, they saw two cats and kittens near a store. "Look, a small family of cats. Just like us, a small family," Yevhenii said to Alla as he hugged her.

Alla dreamed of celebrating Christmas with her boyfriend because Christmas is a family holiday. But their small family was destroyed by a tank shell. "That day I died with you," Alla wrote.

10 days after Yevhenii's death, Alla finally came to accept the unavoidable. She understood that no matter what she did, it wouldn't bring her beloved back. Now she wants only two things: to send as many of those responsible for his death as possible to hell and to continue his memory forever.

This father will never see his newborn daughter. Nataliia lost her husband Vitalii

Vitalii Kyrkach-Antonenko was a well-known activist and Ukrainian defender from the village of Maidan, Donetsk Oblast. At the beginning of the full-scale Russian invasion of Ukraine, he immediately went to defend his motherland.

Nataliia and Vitalii met in Donetsk in 2004 during the presidential elections. Their shared pro-Ukrainian position brought the couple closer. They lived together happily for 18 years until the war took Vitalii's life.

After graduating from university, the couple returned to Sloviansk and started a business. Vitalii read a lot, drew, and took part in pro-Ukrainian events. In 2014, when Russia annexed Ukrainian Crimea and started their war in Donbas, the couple began volunteering. They donated part of their profits to the needs of the army.

"On the first day of the full-scale war, Vitalii went to defend Ukraine. Our country and his love and service to it were always his top priority," Nataliia recalls. She did not even try to persuade her husband not to go to war, because he had to do what he believed was right.

Vitalii Kyrkach-Antonenko fought for 8 months. He served as an infantryman, but together with his comrades he performed other tasks, like mining forest roads close to the enemy's positions in order to prevent the Russians from leaving the encirclement of Ukrainian troops.

On November 8-9, there was very heavy fighting in the Svatove sector. Ukrainian forces were bearing the fury of Russian artillery, armor, and infantry Despite the fact that Vitalii was an ordinary soldier, at that time he was assigned to be the leader of his squad. Vitalii handled his duties bravely. However, on November 9, around 12 o'clock, a shell exploded near the trench where his squad was sheltering. Everyone who was nearby was concussed. A shell fragment struck Vitalii in the head, and his wound was not survivable.

A few days before his death, Vitalii had managed to come visit wife on leave. This meeting was extremely important for them, because they went for an ultrasound scan and found out that they were soon to have a baby girl. In August, when the couple saw each other only once in

Sloviansk, Nataliia became pregnant. They were both so happy holding the ultrasound photo.

> "My heart breaks with devastation and horror at my future life without the brightest person I have ever met. Vitasyk left me the most important gift that can be in this world – a little baby who lives inside me. I hope that in half a year she will be born and look at me with his kind and gentle eyes," Nataliia wrote on her Facebook after the news of her husband's death.

Vitalii Kyrkach-Antonenko was a very handsome man, and his mates even gave him the callsign Krasyvyi (Handsome). But everyone who knew Vitalii will remember him for spiritual beauty: his kindness, generosity, sincerity, and courage.

Unfortunately, Nataliia could not attend her husband's funeral, because it was too dangerous for a pregnant woman to come to Sloviansk, which is located very close to the fighting.

"Not being able to say goodbye to you is unbearable pain and despair. Rest in peace, my gentle sunshine, and come to me in my dreams. I promise to dedicate the rest of my life to our little one and your dreams. And one day, finally, to be by your side. Rest, my love, and I'll watch over your peaceful sleep. And your friends will avenge you," she wrote.

Nataliia is trying to be strong for their daughter. She also decided to name her daughter Vitalina in honor of her father.

Russia killed Daria's husband and father of twins.
Artem, a Ukrainian soldier, fell in Lysychansk

Artem and Daria studied together at the university in Starobilsk, Luhansk Oblast. Daria participated in various youth activities, and Artem was a volunteer and helped the Armed Forces (even before Russia's full-scale invasion in February 2022). The couple met and fell in love thanks to their activism.

"He charmed me with his respect for me as a woman. He treated me very sensitively, and carried me in his arms. It was just like in the movies," Daria recalls.

Artem and Daria got married on August 27, 2020,, and their twins – Myroslava and Emiliia were born on February 20, 2021. A year later, the family celebrated the girls' birthday. Artem took leave for this time to spend more time with his family, and then go on vacation. But on February 22, he received a call from his commander and was urgently called to duty. He was given 2 days to prepare.

On the morning of the full-scale invasion, Daria's mother woke Artem up, telling him, "Tiomchyk, get up, the war has started!" He started getting calls and calling people. His men were already there, and they had already taken fire.

When Daria hugged Artem for the last time, she begged him to stay. But he said: "No. You don't understand. If I stay now, our future is only Russia. How will I look the girls in the eyes if I stay?"

In early March, the city of Starobilsk, where Daria lived with her children, fell under Russian occupation. Enemy soldiers began to detain and interrogate locals. As the wife of a border guard, it was dangerous for Daria to stay in the city. However, it was also frightening to leave, because the Russians fired upon evacuation buses.

One day, Russian soldiers came to Artem's parents' house. At that moment, Daria and her daughters were alone there. She grabbed her children in her arms and ran out of the house. They managed to escape unnoticed through neighboring yards. Daria still remembers how it was raining, her daughters were crying, and she held them close to her and ran through the puddles.

Daria and Artem talked whenever possible. There was often poor connection where he was serving. Artem insisted that Daria and all their family members leave Starobilsk. He was ready to pay any price for it.

On May 8, Artem had his 26th birthday. There was no contact with him, so no one was able to call to wish him a happy birthday. But on May 9 he called Daria himself. Surprisingly, the connection at that time was very good. Daria was able to see her beloved's face as clearly as she had ever seen in three months of war. Artem told his wife that he was now in Lysychansk and promised to call the next day. But the next day, it was not Artem who called Daria, but another officer of the border service. Daria immediately realized what had happened: her husband had been killed. A Russian shell hit the plant where Artem was on duty.

Artem was buried on May 20 in Dnipro at the Krasnopilske Cemetery. Daria was not able to come to the funeral, as she was not able to leave for Ukrainian-controlled territory until June 20.

Daria and her children could not leave the occupied zone for a very long time, as she wanted to reach free Ukraine, though not via Russia. She wanted to take all her husband's awards and medals with her, so it would be too dangerous to pass through Russian checkpoints, as they searched everyone.

Although Daria's path was difficult and risky, she eventually reached Kharkiv. Then she immediately went to Dnipro and visited her husband's grave. Daria moved from Dnipro to Rivne Oblast. It is too difficult now for her to live in the city where her husband is buried.

> "My children were left without their father. I want them to know what their dad was like when they got older. What a friend, companion, and protector he was. I will do everything to make my girls proud to say their last name," says Daria.

Artem Hurtovyi dreamed that his daughters Emiliia and Myroslava would live in Ukraine, speak Ukrainian, and love their country. Daria has promised to fulfill her husband's wish.

"I am young, I am a widow." Nadiia's husband was killed in the war. She tells their story

I am 38 and a widow. My husband died in the war. Yes, at war, in the 21st century, in the center of Europe. This is who I am now.

I don't feel like myself anymore. My body does not fully belong to me. I either don't eat or eat too much. The taste of the food is lean and bland. Periodically, I catch myself thinking that I am eating what my husband loved.

I am "heavy" and "wooly," like a clumsy toy stuffed with straw. It's hard for me to move my legs, sometimes I cannot hold things in my hands. Even the phone feels too heavy.

I'm a widow, I'm still young. But I don't feel beautiful anymore. I can no longer reconcile myself to my external flaws, now I only see them. I cannot be beautiful anymore. Not because I don't want to. I don't have the strength for it.

I am like a torn and faded pumpkin left alone in the field. Maybe not completely alone, because there are enough torn pumpkins in the field, I am not the only one who will never hug her husband again.

My son is growing up so fast and his dad isn't there to watch anymore. He is growing and I don't have enough resources to give him the attention he needs right now. I've frozen. I've stopped. I'm confused. I'm petrified.

People clap my shoulder and give me words of support and gratitude. Time is running out. There are fewer people and in the end I am alone in a dark, empty apartment. Everyone goes to their families, but I no longer have one.

Sometimes I forget that he died and I live the way I lived before, in calm worry. But reality still insists. It will never be the same again. No one will ever take away my sorrow, sadness, uncertainty, bitterness, and anger.

I'll never forget who did this. Who stole my dreams, gutted my happiness, destroyed my life.

The only thing I really want now is for the bullets of our soldiers to reach the bodies of the enemy, for the artillery to hit even more precisely, for the enemy to be destroyed without pity and pain, without compassion and remorse.

I want Russia to not exist anymore. And no one will make this happen except you (the Ukrainian military). Yes, at the cost of our own lives, yes, at the cost of our widowhood, yes, at the cost of the postponed happy future of our children. We will restore everything after victory, we will restore ourselves. We will grow our nation again. As our mothers and grandmothers did for centuries before us.

Perhaps in that distant dreamy future, we torn and faded pumpkins will want to live a little and find ourselves and our new meanings. Armed Forces of Ukraine, bring this day closer for us."

***

Nadiia and her husband met in 2015 at military training. Then they worked as paramedics. In 2018, Nadia's husband was offered a job as a software developer in France, and the couple moved to Marseille.

Last year, they had a son. But Nadiia's husband always said that there would be a big war and was preparing for it. He was a warrior in spirit. Nadiia could not stop him, so she let him go. He was a platoon commander in a rifle regiment and was killed in Kharkiv Oblast.

10-year-old Nastia was killed by the Russians. The story of the Stoliuk family from a village near Kyiv

Liubov Stoliuk met the first explosions of the full-scale Russian invasion in her home village of Shybene in Bucha District. The loud noise frightened her children, and 10-year-old Nastia did not leave her mother's side all day. Liubov was also worried about her 21-year-old daughter Masha, who is on the autism spectrum. Any change in Masha's routines could cause her to react unpredictably, and now war had arrived.

On the evening of February 24, 2022, Liubov decided to move her family to her brother Mykola's house on another street. The next day, they saw columns of Russian vehicles moving through the village.

On March 1, Liubov and her children sat down to eat. Suddenly, they heard the sounds of gunfire. Mykola shouted for them to lie down on the floor. All four of them hid in the room, thinking that it would be safer there. At one point, Liubov heard a whistle, and something flew into the house. Her brother was already wounded, and he started shouting, "To the basement!."

Mykola and Liubov grabbed Masha and dragged her out of the damaged house. When they hid her in the basement, they realized that Nastia had not come with them. When Liubov pulled her daughter towards her, she realized that she was mortally wounded.

> "It was hot running down my hand, I immediately understood that it was blood. I started shouting: "They killed Nastia!." She was hit in the right temple, and her brain came out," Liubov said.

Mykola was hit in the head with the same shell that killed Nastia. He could not receive professional medical attention due to the occupation, so they treated the wound as best they could.

After the deadly shelling, it was too dangerous for the Stoliuk family to stay at home. Besides, everything there reminded them of Nastia's death.

The family went to their friends' dacha. A few days later, Russian soldiers visited them. They were looking for "the mother of the murdered girl." They had already been told that the child had died. They started apologizing and saying they did not mean to do it. "Your little girl died because of your own people. If we hadn't been provoked, this wouldn't have happened," the Russians said.

Russian soldiers later offered to help Liubov with Nastia's burial. However, there were tanks at the local cemetery at the time, and it was impossible to bury her there. Then one tank was moved, and Liubov, Mykola, and another neighbor took Nastia's body to the cemetery. They reached the old collective farm, and then shelling started again. They had to bury Nastia girl right there, and then dig up and bury her once again in the cemetery.

Nastia was ultimately buried three times. The last one was after exhumation. "When the prosecutor's office came to us from Kyiv, they said that Nastia might have to be dug up again. I said that they could immediately bury me with her. Well, can you imagine that I would have to see my child like that for the fourth time? I called the investigator, and asked about it, she said that the request should be made by the prosecutor's office or the court. I hope we won't have to dig up Nastia for a fourth time," Liubov said.

His wife was kidnapped and murdered by the Russians. The story of Ihor from Trostianets

Ihor Ivanov is a resident of Trostianets, Sumy Oblast. The Russian occupation came as a surprise to him. "I remember looking out the window in the morning, and seeing tanks driving in front of my windows. There was equipment, armored vehicles, and fuel trucks."

Ihor's children lived on a neighboring street, so they often went to visit each other. One day his wife went out somewhere and did not come back. And then the mobile connection disappeared. Electricity was turned off, and the cellular towers did not work. Ihor walked and looked for her wherever he could.

Three days after the city was liberated by the Ukrainian military, the police station in Trostianets resumed operations. Ihor came to them to make an official report about his wife's disappearance. Two months later, he received the terrible call to come identify her.

His wife's body was found accidentally, buried half a meter underground. Although it was difficult to recognize her, Ihor saw unmistakable indications that it was indeed her.

Ihor recalls that on the evening of his wife's disappearance, another 10-15 people were detained. He doesn't know what exactly happened then. According to the doctors, Ihor's wife was shot in the head.

"My wife worked in commerce. At that time we were growing and selling flowers. We had a small flower business that had just started to develop. The whole of Trostianets knew her. She also worked in the hardware store for a long time," Ihor said.

Ihor doesn't know why his wife was detained. Perhaps she was out after the 5:00 pm curfew that the Russian occupiers had imposed. At that time, moving around the city was risky.

Unlike his children, Ihor remained in Trostianets during the entire occupation. He kept waiting for his wife, and hoped that she would return. Now he is waiting for the return of his children who evacuated abroad. Perhaps they'll come home closer to spring when it gets warmer.

This text is based on testimony collected by the Kharkiv Human Rights Protection Group.

Surviving Atrocities: Tales of Life Under Russian Occupation

"People were kidnapped from streets and cafés."
Anastasiia from Berdiansk tells her story of occupation and evacuation

During the first days of the great war, Anastasiia'a family packed their things and went to her mother's so that they could all be together. The three of them had three animals. Nothing was clear, they were constantly hearing explosions outside the city, and they were following the news nonstop.

They could not have even imagined that after two days of the war, on February 26, the Russians would enter their city and cut them off from the world. On that day, the Russians blew up the railway bridge in Vasylivka and bombed the roads, making it impossible for Ukrainians to leave.

In early March, all communication was completely cut off. Anastasiia and her family felt like they were hostages in their own city and their own home. Vehicles with Z markings were all over the city, as were Russian armed soldiers.

For the first few days, people bravely went to rallies and tried to fight on their own, but by early March, Russian paddy wagons had been parked in a row near the Berdiansk embankment to stop any rallies. Russian Rosgvardia, in addition to soldiers, began patrolling the city.

Then, the occupiers began kidnapping people from their apartments and from the street. Anastasiia's family saw a man dragged from a cafe in the center of Berdiansk and taken away to an unknown place. People lived in constant fear, like an endless Groundhog Day.

Only on April 3 did the family manage to leave on an evacuation bus. They traveled more than 14 hours from Berdiansk to Zaporizhzhia (200 km). Anastasiia and her family were stopped at every checkpoint for inspection by the Russians.

Russians checked their belongings and searched for tattoos. They mockingly asked if Anastasiia's family was carrying grenades, and who was forcing them to go to Zaporizhzhia. Russians believed that someone was forcing them to go to Ukraine. As Anastasiia and her family drove, they saw an endless line of destroyed houses and burnt cars. The Russians were checking phones – Ukrainians had to delete all their messengers and photos so that they would not find anything. Some people's phones were taken away. It was impossible to photograph anything along the way, as the Russians were checking. There were sections of the road where it was impossible to get off the bus at all, as there were mines all around.

They are now 5,000 km from Berdiansk. They have quite deliberately moved away from this horror, but the fear of loud sounds and planes has stayed with them for a long time, as have the nightmares. In their minds, they still don't feel like they are finally free. "Many thanks to those kind people who have supported us during this period. People are what matters," Anastasiia says.

"The nights were the scariest for me." Life during the siege of Mariupol

On March 8, Mariupol no longer had electricity, heating, communications, gas, or local government officials remaining (with a handful of very brave exceptions). Maryna Holovnova and her family slept in a windowless room and hoped that the two walls around them would protect them from Russian bombs.

To be more precise, they almost did not sleep at all, because they could hardly breathe from the fear and cold. From the way shockwaves shook the walls and furniture in their apartment and the hum of planes over the city. "The nights were the scariest for me. When I finally saw the light through the doorway, it became a little easier. It meant we had survived until morning," said Maryna.

After waking up on the morning of March 8, Maryna spent 40 minutes trying to boil a pot of water using scrap wood near the door to her apartment building. It was -8°C outside and snowing. At 8 am, as usual, Maryna's family went to the since-destroyed Mariupol Drama Theater to see their friends and learn at least some news. It was quite close, but on the way they had to take cover several times due to the threat of shelling.

The sirens in Mariupol were never turned on. Maryna heard them for the first time when she reached Zaporizhzhia on March 17.

"In Mariupol, we learned about the threat of an air raid from the sound of the Russian warplanes themselves. We hid and listened for the first bomb to fall, then the second, because the bombers would carry two of them. Then we waited a few more minutes in case the plane was not alone. If it was quiet, it was possible to go out and continue to do business. Even children knew this routine," Maryna said.

> *"Near the drama theater, people stood for hours in the cold, waiting for information: what is happening in the country and in the city, and whether there will be a green evacuation corridor today or tomorrow."*

In the afternoon, soldiers came to the theater and brought diapers, blankets, and cookies to the children from what they had managed to collect around the city. They also handed out leaflets with news. As always, they cheerfully told people about the situation on the front line: "We will beat them back soon. We are doing everything we can so that you all can leave."

A new friend of Maryna's family, who would soon save them, brought a bouquet of flowers. It was March 8, celebrated as Women's Day in Ukraine. "I held those flowers in my hands, and people were surprised. They came up and asked just to smell them. They didn't believe that the flowers were real, that there was still something of normal life left in this seemingly forgotten city," Maryna recalls. Later, the police also came to the Drama Theater. A man asked one of them what he should do with his neighbor's dead body. She had gone out into her building's courtyard to warm up food when a shell landed nearby and tore her to pieces. He had put her remains in a bag and took them to a garage.

There was no news about a green corridor that day, so Maryna and her family went back home. They said goodbye to their friends until tomorrow. "Every time I thought that we so easily promised to see each other tomorrow, but there is still half a day and a night ahead, and who knows where the Russians would drop another bomb, and who would live to see that 'tomorrow,'" Holovnova said.

They had to have time to prepare something to eat before darkness and curfew began. There were several fireplaces near the children's playground, and pans, kettles, and pots set on refrigerator racks. Someone even brought out a bottle of champagne and plastic cups. It was March 8. There was only champagne for the women – the men just smiled and said kind words.

One of Maryna's neighbors suddenly said that his son was preparing a poem for the holiday in kindergarten and that it would be a pity if no one heard it. The boy climbed onto the highest horizontal bar in the middle of the courtyard. People gathered around and fell silent, and he began to recite the poem loudly and clearly.

The poem was in Ukrainian, about his mother, spring, and flowers. The last line was about our beautiful Ukrainian home. Everyone stood in silence for a few more seconds, and then began to applaud. The boy was extremely proud of himself. Someone gave him a bit of scarce chocolate candy.

After March 8, the Russians began shelling the center of Mariupol almost non-stop. Shells hit neighboring houses, killing Maryna's neighbors and burning down their cars and apartments. Her family could no longer stay in their apartment on the fourth floor.

On March 15, they took their backpacks, food, and water to go find a new shelter. They went around the surrounding houses with basements. A man came out of one basement and told them that there was no more room there. He advised them to go to the Drama Theater, but every meter of space on all three floors and in the basement was already occupied. Volunteers had stopped letting new people in.

Maryna remembered about an industrial college nearby. It was a two-story building from the late 19th century with thick, dark brick walls.

"We went to check if people were hiding there. In the hall there were huge windows with wooden frames, some already without glass. We had to move from one end of the corridor to the other quickly, in order not to be hit by deadly shards of glass in the event of a close strike," Maryna said.

After walking around the building, it became clear that nobody had been inside since the beginning of the attack on Mariupol. For Maryna's family, it was the last shelter in Mariupol.

"We stayed there with our friends, taking a small room without windows under the stairs. It belonged to the cleaner. There was a half-empty can of instant coffee. It was such happiness! We made a fire in the courtyard, boiled water and allowed ourselves a cup of coffee each," Holovnova recalls.

> "At night, everyone was unbearably cold, and it was buzzing like never before. Nobody could sleep. Around 2 am, another bomb fell nearby, 200 meters from the college. The Russians hit the central department store on Myru Avenue."

The massive college building stood strong like a fortress. For the first time in many nights, the walls around Maryna did not shake, and this created at least an illusion of safety. However, the windows in the hall did not hold up, and glass fell from them onto the floor. In the morning, everything was covered with sharp glass shards.

The next day, the Russians dropped a 500-kilogram bomb on the Mariupol Drama Theater. The circle had closed. There were no safe places left. Fortunately, unlike some other residents of the city, Maryna and her family managed to leave for a safer place.

"I will remember that night for the rest of my life." Mariia and her child lived through Russian occupation and bombing

Mariia Ivaniuk had prepared in advance for a possible full-scale Russian invasion. A few weeks before February 24, she already had bags packed with everything she needed. She always took documents and a backpack with a basic supply of food, medicine, and other important things with her when she went out.

Mariia checked all the air raid shelters near her house, and was worried every time she took her son to daycare. She and her husband thought out a plan for what to do and where to go if war started. Her diligent preparations stemmed from the fact that her father and her husband had fought against the Russians in Donbas since 2014, so they were well aware of what Russian aggression was.

On February 24, Mariia and her husband woke up to explosions. They immediately understood where they were coming from. Her husband got a phone call and they knew that Russia had indeed started its full-scale war.

Although Mariia and her son had planned to immediately evacuate to western Ukraine, they first stopped by her mother in the village of Buzova, Kyiv Oblast. Her two sisters, her nephew, and her younger brother had gathered at her parents' house. Mariia convinced everyone to move on urgently because Russian troops would advance towards Kyiv along the Zhytomyr highway, where their village is located.

However, Mariia's mother did not want to leave her home, so her sisters hesitated. Mariia could not leave herself, because she did not have a car. Unfortunately, before they could get to safety, fierce fighting erupted near Buzova, and the village fell under occupation.

February 28 was the scariest night of Mariia's life: "I will remember that night for the rest of my life. I was afraid not of my own death, but for my son, brother, and nephew who were with us. I had a feeling of incredible guilt for not taking them out earlier, for not saving them. I felt terrible because I didn't listen to myself, I didn't do everything I knew and understood before the war, and now they could die or get hurt," she recalls.

Mariia and her family sat in the cellar where her great-grandmother and grandmother once hid from the Nazis during World War II. Now they were hiding from Russia there. The place was so humid that they could not make their lighter work, and a candle brought in from the street would immediately go out. The lime on the walls got into the humid air, and then into their noses and lungs. There was little oxygen because the cellar was small and there were many people. At first, Mariia and her relatives thought that they were having panic attacks, but then they realized that it was the lack of oxygen that made it difficult to breathe.

The concrete walls, floor, and ceiling also amplified the sounds of the explosions and gunshots that constantly rang out above. Cracks began to appear in the thick concrete ceiling, so Mariia and her family were afraid that it would fall on them. The ground shook under and around them from the Russian shelling.

> "At this moment, you clearly understand that life can really end at any moment. And it is not a fear of death, but a fear of losing every moment. Just wasting your time. That night I felt faith again. Faith in an incredible power that cares for this world. We traditionally call this God, but other religions have many other names. I believed in something of my own. And I am grateful to this Power that helped us and continues to take care of us," says Mariia.

Although Mariia did not know if she would survive that night, and even said goodbye to all her friends in a Facebook post just in case, the shelling stopped and their basement survived. Then Mariia and her 3-year-old son Yura managed to leave for Lviv Oblast.

Unfortunately, after the experience, Mariia's son developed severe post-traumatic stress. Even in safety, he was frightened by every noise and fell to the ground, covering his ears with his hands. Yura was also greatly distressed by the sounds of air raid sirens. Pained by her son's suffering, Mariia decided to go abroad. They now live temporarily in Denmark and are hoping for Ukraine's victory to come soon.

"Russians were shooting people at random." Tetiana survived the occupation of Borodianka with her family

Tetiana Klihunova from Borodianka survived the occupation of her town together with her family. She had to communicate with Russian soldiers and bury her neighbors in her own garden. She admits that she kept herself sane and alive by busying herself with household chores, while her husband managed to make a washing machine that worked without electricity.

On February 23, Tetiana discussed the possibility of a major war with her friend. It had seemed scarcely believable, but when she turned on her television the following day, she heard that Kyiv was being bombed. After that, the oil depot in Borodianka was set on fire and, later, Russian soldiers entered the town.

Tetiana lived with other family members during the occupation: her husband, daughter, son-in-law, her brother-in-law and his partner, two grandchildren, and a nephew. Tetiana's brother-in-law stayed at home at first, but the Russian military came to his house and forced him out.

Russians approached Tetiana and asked her where Ukrainian policemen and soldiers were living. However, she replied that this was a peaceful street and that the only people living there were pensioners.

Every morning, Russian armored personnel carriers would drive down the street where Tetiana's family lived, carrying many soldiers with automatic weapons. Every morning and every evening, the Russians would patrol the streets of Borodianka. Local residents were very frightened and tried not to leave their homes under any circumstances.

> "I told my grandchildren, 'Don't get involved – how do we know what's on their mind? One of them might just decide to shoot someone out of boredom,'" Tetiana recalls.

She also said that the Russian soldiers had drunk all the vodka from the local stores within a week, after which they had run amok, shooting people at random. Tetiana saw a glow from Bucha and Irpin and she realized that terrible battles were raging there. It was then that Tetiana's family went down into the basement. They had collected their belongings, documents, and money, but they could not leave

Borodianka. They had no time to refuel their car before the Russian occupiers surrounded the town.

When the Russians began to bomb Borodianka, Tetiana did her best to distract herself with work around the house, cleaning, and cooking food. Her husband even made a new washing machine from an old one that could operate without electricity by constantly turning a handle. After eight missiles landed in Borodianka, the town was left completely dark.

Tetiana and her son-in-law organized a makeshift mortuary in their own garden. They carried their dead neighbors from nearby yards and streets so that they could be buried later. However, Tetiana explained that some people would never receive a proper burial. When an aerial bomb hit one house in Borodianka, its inhabitants' remains were never found. They were simply blown to pieces.

Fortunately, Tetiana's house survived, with only the garage, chicken coop, and summer kitchen taking damage. She witnessed Russian soldiers looting neighboring houses. "I was going outside when I saw a truck approaching. They loaded it up and drove away, and this was happening everywhere, again and again."

After the full-scale invasion, Russians have simply ceased to exist for Tetiana. Their crimes were inhuman, she says.

This text is based on testimony collected by the Kharkiv Human Rights Protection Group.

"We didn't have the medicines we needed." Serhii survived the Russian occupation of Izium

Serhii Dubinskyi, a native of the Izium, Kharkiv Oblast, has had health problems since childhood and remains disabled. He received welfare payments and worked as a security guard at a sports complex, bringing him enough money to support his sick mother and himself.

At 11 am on July 14, he was returning home from the market. Izium was already occupied by Russian forces, but they wanted to destroy as much of the city as they could, and continued to shell it from time to time.

On the previous day, Serhii's father-in-law was injured by a landmine. Enemy aircraft had littered them across almost a third of the central part of the city and surrounding areas. Fortunately, he survived, but suffered a leg wound.

It was not safe to be outside, at home or even the shelters, but Serhii had to get to his old mother, who was waiting for him.

The first explosion was a reasonable distance away and he was left unscathed. But then cluster bomblets came raining down. A blast wave knocked Serhii to the ground. He was unable to get back up as shell fragments had pierced his left thigh. However, he found the strength to move on his elbows and one knee to some nearby houses.

People helped him at the first entrance, giving him something to drink, treating his wounds, and bandaging him as best they could. When the bombing stopped, Serhii was taken away by an ambulance. Ukrainian medics continued saving lives throughout the incident, where at least 14 people were injured. The number of dead is unknown.

> "They did it on purpose: they fired at the education department, kindergartens, schools and the pension fund building. The Russian troops did this, even though they had been stationed in the city for a long time. They were just having fun destroying old buildings," Serhii said.

In the central district hospital, doctors treated Serhii's wounds and took an X-ray. He was given a wheelchair, on which he finally reached his mother. Neighbors with a car drove him to the medical center for his wounds to be dressed. The wound has since healed, but not without nerve damage.

"We didn't have the medicines we needed during the occupation. I began receiving proper treatment only after the Armed Forces liberated the city, when the necessary equipment and medicines were brought to the hospital and medical specialists returned," Serhii explained.

Serhii also added that it would take several days to relate all the unforgettable horrors that the Russians had perpetrated in Izium.

Serhii now lives with his mother in her house, with three dogs in their yard. Communication problems, a lack of power, and the cold have made people more resilient as they search for insulation materials, basic hygiene products, and food. However, people there believe in the best and are delighted to have been liberated by Ukraine.

This text is based on testimony collected by the Kharkiv Human Rights Protection Group.

"They put all the villagers in the school basement."
Anzhelika tells the story of Yahidne

While the village was under occupation, Russian soldiers forced almost all the residents of Yahidne into the basement of its school. Phones and valuables were confiscated. It was nearly impossible to breathe in the basement, but people were allowed outside at most once a day.

Anzhelika Pretko and her family were among those held in the school basement.

> "At first, me and my family – my mother, father, and grandparents – hid in our basement at home. But on March 5, at around 4 pm, Russian soldiers broke into our home and forced us into the school basement. I studied at this school from 1st to 9th grade," Anzhelika explained.

In a panic, the Anzhelika's family managed to take some essential items, such as medicine, documents, and some food. When Anzhelika arrived at the school basement, more than half of the village was already there, including small children, the elderly, the bedridden, and the disabled. Everyone came to the village because they thought it would be safer here than in the city. How wrong they were.

At first, the occupiers did not take people's belongings, but after two or three days, they started taking phones. Anzhelika's grandparents were sick, and the conditions in the basement were unbearable for them. Not only that, but the Russians were not feeding anyone. All the people had to eat was what they had taken with them. The number of people in the basement made for a suffocating atmosphere. With each passing day, the health of Anzhelika's grandparents deteriorated further. In the end, their legs became almost paralyzed and they grew more and more confused. They could not understand what was happening or where they were.

With their condition so serious, Anzhelika and her parents decided to risk taking them home. Anzhelika's father asked his fellow villagers and they helped. However, the next day, when the occupiers allowed Anzhelika and her brother to go home for just half an hour to gather some things, they found their grandfather dead. He was lying there, no longer breathing. He was 70 years old.

As of 11 March, about 5 people had died in the school basement. The people asked the Russians to allow them to go and bury them.

The next day, Anzhelika went to the cemetery with her fellow villagers. Russian vehicles drove by. Just a few minutes later, the shelling began. Anzhelika had no time to bury her grandfather.

She realized she had been wounded in the back and leg. Her father was also wounded in the leg; both of them could hardly walk. Anzhelika's mother was also injured, but she could move and run, at least.

They escaped the cemetery as best they could and returned to the school basement, because there were military doctors there, who administered first aid and tended to their wounds. Over the course of the following days, they dressed wounds and removed stitches.

All this time, Anzhelika's grandmother remained at home, where all the windows and the roof of their house had been badly damaged. She also had nothing to eat. Anzhelika's family was no longer allowed to go and visit her grandmother. She said that she ate what the soldiers brought her from time to time.

On March 30, the occupiers once again locked the people in the basement. They simply locked the door and refused to let anyone out. The people would normally sit there for several days, and the Russians would allow them out occasionally to breathe fresh air.

This time, however, the people heard the enemy equipment starting to move away. Over the course of the day, they left Yahidne, and the next day Ukrainian soldiers arrived. They checked all the houses, cleared the streets, and let the people return to their homes.

Immediately after the village was liberated, Ukrainian soldiers took Anzhelika's father to the hospital, because he was still unable to walk. Anzhelika and her family evacuated to relatives in a safer location.

This text is based on testimony collected by the Kharkiv Human Rights Protection Group.

"Russia is worse than a horde." Mykola survived the Russian occupation of Moshchun

Mykola understood that Russia could start a full-scale war. He had been thinking about it since 2014, when Russian troops invaded Donbas and occupied Crimea.

When Mykola woke up on February 24, 2022, he did not immediately find out that the war had begun. He realized it when he saw helicopters flying over his village. Women and children were standing on the street, watching the Russians advance. Mykola asked his fellow villagers to get out of the streets and hide. Enemy helicopters were flying to Hostomel, and launched strikes there in order to land troops.

Meanwhile, Mykola packed his emergency suitcase and collected his documents. He and his family dragged their beds into the basement. Mykola's wife, his daughter, son-in-law, and grandchildren all took shelter there. They arrived during lulls in the shelling. Mykola himself did not hide in the basement.

The Russians bombed Moshchun very often, especially in the final days of the occupation. Drones flew overhead day and night. Mykola's wife, daughter, and grandchildren evacuated from the village, while he and his son-in-law remained behind. Local men helped the 72nd Brigade, carried ammunition, and blew up bridges. Mykola prepared coffee and tea for Ukrainian defenders.

From March 4 to 10, heavy shelling began in the part of the village where Mykola's house was. First, an enemy shell hit the workshop near the house. Others then landed in his house, his brother's house, and another neighbor's house. Everything instantly caught fire and burned furiously.

Fortunately, Mykola was not at home at that time. He had a two-story house with a bathroom, boiler, refrigerator, freezer, four TVs, a computer, and a laptop. Mykola's daughter enjoys baking, so there were a lot of kitchen appliances at home. Many of Mykola's tools burned up in his workshop. Only its walls remained.

One of Mykola's neighbors wanted to take his mother out of the village, but when he went to start his car, it was hit by an enemy mortar.

Another neighbor was killed by a shell fragment when he climbed out of his basement. The Russians shot three more of Mykola's acquaintances.

Mykola's plans for the future are to rebuild and live on, and to be happy with his children and grandchildren. He has held ill-will toward Russians since 2015. He has a cousin living in Russia, who said in 2015 that Russian troops would come to Ukraine and "protect" him. After these words, Mykola stopped talking to her.

"Russia is a horde! Even worse than a horde," Mykola says.

This text is based on testimony collected by the Kharkiv Human Rights Protection Group.

Surviving the bomb strike. The story of Larysa from Borodianka

Larysa Tyshchenko was born and has lived all her life in Borodianka. On March 1, 2022, a Russian airstrike destroyed her apartment.

Larysa recalls how, on February 26, Russian troops had tried to break through to the center of Borodianka, only to be stopped by the local Territorial Defense unit. The Russians returned on February 27 with tanks, shelling indiscriminately. They fired at residential buildings and a family of five all died as a result of a direct hit on their house.

> "Russian soldiers were sitting on armored personnel carriers and shooting at civilians who had no time to flee. They were simply gunned down. Every day from February 27, we were forced to sit in the basement of our five-storey building. At night, we could still go up to our apartment to spend the night and cook food, because the gas supply was still intact. However, on March 1, the occupiers began shelling Borodianka from the air for the first time," Larysa explains.

First, they bombed two houses near the entrance to Borodianka. At the time, Larysa was sitting in her basement, but the shockwave threw people across the room.

"Everything appeared to have calmed down in the evening, so we decided that we could at least go out and cook. We also began to take out things that we needed to spend the night in the basement. I was in my apartment, with the kettle on and getting ready, dressing in the corridor, when I suddenly heard the roar of a plane. I immediately understood that it was coming from the direction of the Zdvyzh River and heading straight for me. I just hid behind the wall; there was nowhere else to go. I did not have time to leave the apartment and just waited. I remember the impact: everything was covered in smoke and so much dust that it was impossible to breathe. I realized that I was alive, but I had been knocked down by my wardrobe. It was then that I heard the plane's second approach, this time coming from the other side," Larysa recalls.

There was no way of leaving the apartment through the front door, because it was blocked by rubble. Men from a Territorial Defense unit arrived at the scene and told Larysa to make her way through the rubble to the next entrance along and try to go down the stairs that were still intact. Larysa succeeded and, thankfully, escaped unscathed.

Nothing is known about many residents who were at home at the time of the airstrike; not even body fragments have been found. "It's frightening and hard to comprehend. Personally, I have lost everything: my possessions, my apartment, and all my documents. Not a single photograph was left, and it is almost impossible to restore my past life," says Larysa.

Larysa is convinced that the Russians dropped bombs on residential buildings intentionally, because there was nothing else in the vicinity other than apartment buildings and a kindergarten.

In the days that followed, Larysa hid in the basement of her neighbor Mariia. Throughout this time, convoys of Russian vehicles were passing through Borodianka. It appeared that the enemy had arranged these bombing raids to prevent the Territorial Defense from shooting at their equipment and stopping them from capturing the village.

A little later, Larysa called her son and told him she was still alive. Her children had thought she was gone. Larysa asked her son to take her away from Borodianka, so, once the Russian convoys had passed through, her son came and took her to the outskirts of the town, where she and her in-laws hid in a basement for several days.

On March 6, when it was reported that the Russians had begun bombing the bridges, Larysa and her relatives left Borodianka. They traveled across Ukraine, spending the night wherever they stopped, in kindergartens and health farms, before settling first in Zakarpattia and then with friends in an unfinished house in Zhmerynka. Larysa and her children were evacuated there until May.

On February 24, Larysa had asked her children to come from Kyiv to Borodianka. "Thank God they didn't come, because their room at the apartment in Borodianka was completely destroyed by the bomb. It would have been their grave," says Larysa.

"My classmate Tania Lykhno's husband was shot on the street. He was walking down the street and asked some Russian soldiers for a smoke. They gave him a cigarette, he turned around, and they just shot him in the back. He lay there until night time, then even got up and made it home by himself, but he was dead the following morning," Larysa said.

People who remained under the occupation throughout that time told Larysa that the Russian snipers would pass the time by climbing to the roof of one of the residential buildings in Borodianka and opening fire on civilians, shooting at their feet.

Larysa Tyshchenko now lives in her mother's apartment in Borodianka. She is happy that she and her family are alive. There are worse things in life than losing an apartment and having the power cut off.

This text is based on testimony collected by the Kharkiv Human Rights Protection Group.

Journeys to safety: Evacuation Chronicles

Bullets stuck in her body. Myroslava escaped death while leaving Irpin with her daughter

On March 7, 2022, Myroslava Svistovych and her daughter Lada managed to escape from the occupation of Irpin, Kyiv Oblast. At that time, there was heavy fighting between Russian and Ukrainian forces in the city, so it was too dangerous to stay at home.

The evacuation from Irpin was also highly dangerous and risky. Myroslava and her daughter were almost killed trying to leave the city.

"Our car sped down Tyschenko Street and turned onto Universitetska Street. At that time, a friend from Kyiv called me. "Taya, we are in a hurry to evacuate, I will call you back later." I turned off my phone and saw the windshield of our car had been blown away by the gunfire...," Myroslava recalls.

The next moments happened in slow motion. She turned her head to the right, where her daughter Lada was sitting, and saw that the window by her head had also shattered into pieces.

Instantly, like in a movie, Myroslava shouted at her daughter to duck. However, Lada could not do so, because on her lap was a large carrier with their cat, which had been injured the day before.

This may have saved her life, because if she had ducked, the bullet that hit her stomach may instead have hit her head or neck. However, at that moment, Myroslava did not know that her daughter had been hit.

After a few more seconds, Myroslava saw their driver slowly lean to the left, open the door, and fall out of the car. The car continued to move at a fairly high speed without a driver.

> "I don't drive a car and I'm not a superman who can move from the back seat of the car to the driver's seat in seconds, so the only thing that came to my mind was that we also needed to jump out. Besides, they could have kept shooting at us. Therefore, I said to my daughter, "Lada, jump out!" Myroslava recounts.

After taking everything that could have trapped her daughter in the car (2 backpacks, a laptop, and a bag with documents), Myroslava jumped out. At that moment, the car reached the left edge of the road, where the asphalt ended and the ground began. Thus, her landing was fortunately relatively soft.

"Actually, I don't remember how I ended up on the ground, but I didn't get a single scratch. It seems like something I had done a thousand times before. The only thing I felt was the car turning from my jump and going to the opposite side of the road diagonally, passing over my right leg before that. But it wasn't painful at all," she recalls.

As she laid on the ground, Myroslava saw the car moving away from her and waited for her daughter to jump out of it. But she did not. Finally, the car drove into a ditch on the right side of the road, and then Lada got out of it with a cat carrier.

Once she made sure that her daughter was alive, Myroslava began looking around in all directions to understand what was happening around her. She saw three Russian soldiers coming towards them. She again started shouting to her daughter to lie down next to the car, while she continued to assess the situation and think about how to reach her daughter on the other side of the road.

"The distance between us was about 40 meters across the asphalt road. If it were regular ground, I could have crawled, but crawling on asphalt didn't seem like the best idea. I decided that I would just try to run over, and if they shot me, I would fall," Myroslava says.

Crouched down, she ran to her daughter, and the Russians did not shoot her. Lying down next to her daughter, Myroslava told her that they would probably have to let their cat go, because they had to run away, and it would be more difficult while carrying their cat. But Lada flatly refused to leave the cat behind.

Since they could not run away, Myroslava continued to think about what to do next. She decided to call someone to tell them what happened so that in the worst-case scenario, their relatives would at least know how they had died.

Since Myroslava's main phone was already dead, she took out another one, which she had bought just a week ago for her new business. It did not have any personal contacts, but it was fully charged. She asked her daughter to give her the piece of paper on which her husband had written important phone numbers.

Myroslava called her husband's friend Serhii and told him everything.

At a certain point, she had to hang up, because the Russians were coming very close to Myroslava and Lada.

"At this point, the computer in my head was going through all possible options for what we could do and how they would react to it. I looked at the soldiers, then at my daughter, who was lying next to the carrier with the cat, and I understood that her life depended on my actions and words," Myroslava recalls.

A scream could provoke the occupiers to aggression, and a plea for mercy could prompt them to deny it. Then Myroslava remembered a situation from her life and decided to ask the Russians for help. Usually, those to whom you show trust and ask for help will not do you harm.

So Myroslava raised her hand and said in Russian, "Please help." She said it as if she was asking them to help her lift a heavy suitcase. She did not want to show her fear.

Her words surprised the Russian soldiers. They asked her who she was calling. Myroslava lied about calling her husband. The Russians ordered her to drop her phone and stomped on it. Then they asked if Myroslava and her daughter still had phones, and she lied that they did not, even though she still had three phones in her pockets. Luckily, the occupiers did not check.

Next, the Russians asked, "Who are you, and where are you going?" Myroslava answered that they were civilians on their way to evacuate. Eventually, the soldiers let them go.

Myroslava and her daughter went through the forest to Soborna Street. Myroslava carried the cat and the backpacks walking in front, while Lada walked behind her. Since the bullet-torn carrier looked like it was about to fall apart, the daughter stopped Myroslava and forced her to repair it so that the cat wouldn't jump out and run away.

"She did all this with a bullet in her stomach, which I did not even know about, because her injury was covered by her jacket. I did not see that her shirt was covered in blood under her jacket. Later, she said that it was very difficult for her to walk, as if there was a stone in her stomach. She just wanted to sit down and not move. But she had to keep moving to get to the vet, where our injured cat would be saved. She did not tell me a word about her injury," said Myroslava.

On the way, they managed to stop a car that took them to the blown-up Irpin bridge. Then they had to cross the river on the rickety planks laid down underneath the bridge. Volunteers helped them by taking their backpacks and the cat carrier.

Then one of the volunteers asked Lada if she was injured and if she needed to be carried. Lada finally said she was. Only when Lada was put on a stretcher on the other side of the river and the jacket covering the wound was cut open did Myroslava see that her daughter's shirt was covered in blood.

One bullet went through her right breast, and the other lodged in her stomach on the left. Each of these bullets, if they entered a bit further to the right or left, could have been fatal for Lada, as could the bullets that left holes in the hood of Myroslava's jacket.

Later, Myroslava and Lada learned that on March 7, at the same place where they almost died, several more cars were shot. But their passengers were not lucky enough to survive.

Mother and daughter eventually reached Kyiv, where Lada and their cat underwent surgery. The family ended up in an almost empty Kyiv, where most of the population left in the first two days of the war. But after Irpin, which became the capital's key line of defense, Kyiv felt like the safest place on earth for Myroslava and Lada.

Evacuating, returning home, and evacuating again. Kateryna fled the war from Zaporizhzhia with her young son

Even before the full-scale Russian invasion, Kateryna Markova's family knew that there would be an attack, so they were looking for ways to get their little son Markiian out in advance.

On February 21, 2022 Kateryna bought tickets to Antalya for herself, her mother, and her son. To save $100, she bought tickets for February 24, not February 22. They wanted to believe that this trip would be just a quick getaway to somewhere warm.

On the night of February 24, Kateryna and her husband Taras drank wine, watched an episode of Ozark, and went to bed quite late at around 2 am. Their things were packed.

"At 4 am, Marik woke up and just spun for an hour and a half. I was, to be honest, drunk, and I just hugged him, desperately wanting to sleep, because I had to wake up early and go to the airport. Looking ahead – since then, I always look at the news when my son suddenly wakes up at night," Kateryna recalls.

At 7 in the morning, her mother called her and said in a trembling voice: "Katya, baby, did you see the news? We won't make it [to the airport – ed.]."

Kateryna opened the news in shock, and woke up Taras, telling him "We have been attacked, and the whole country is being bombed," and began to repack things from the suitcase they had packed for the trip into their emergency go bag.

Like all Zaporizhzhians, they feared above all that the Russians would bomb the Dnipro Hydroelectric Station. Their house was literally next to it. Therefore, the family decided to move to their relatives on the right bank of the Dnipro with a good basement.

They stayed in that crowded basement for two weeks. Kateryna spent the nights with her son only in the basement. They hardly saw Taras at that point, because he was helping the Ukrainian military.

> "My relatives say that all this time I was a nervous wreck. Personally, I remember almost nothing. Only constant urges to

vomit from nerves. And shame that my friends were volunteering since the first day while I was sitting in the basement with my child. And constant swings from "I have to go somewhere" to "I won't go anywhere from here," recalls Kateryna.

Kateryna and her family made their first attempt to leave on March 5, after the seizure of the Zaporizhzhia Nuclear Power Plant. Half of Zaporizhzhia probably left at that point. But in Dnipropetrovsk Oblast, the family was stuck in a terrible traffic jam, and it was simply impossible to find a room to sleep in. There was overnight frost, not enough fuel, and panic all over the country. Kateryna went crazy and made the call to turn back.

This ended up being the right decision because when Kateryna, her mother, and her son made their second attempt on March 9, the highway was practically empty. They did not know where they were going. Simply to the West of the country.

In Uman, Kateryna asked her followers on Instagram to help her family find shelter. She got a response from a woman named Uliana, who offered Kateryna's family an entire empty house in a village in Ternopil Oblast. Kateryna received other wonderful offers but chose this one because it was closest to the highway, and her sister, who had also evacuated, was also nearby.

Kateryna's family spent almost 2 months in that house in their first evacuation. They waited for May 9 to get a better idea of what lay ahead.

"When we returned to Zaporizhzhia, many people criticized me. But I needed to be with my husband, who had already joined the Armed Forces. All summer, we were at home under constant air raids and the sounds of explosions at night. That was until the real missile terror began in Zaporizhzhia in September. Every night, I started to make a bed for us in the corridor, and almost every night we had to run there," Kateryna says.

When, on the night of Markiian's birthday, a missile struck the place where the family had planned to celebrate, they took it as a conclusive sign that they needed to get out again for a while.

The family left for relatively peaceful Kyiv, which had long since resumed living its usual life. However, as soon as Kateryna arrived there, the first massive bombing of critical infrastructure began. It was October 10, and they spent the nights in the basement again.

Renting expensive housing in Kyiv and living without electricity did not seem like a very good idea to Kateryna, so they returned to Zaporizhzhia again with a plan to look for a place where they could spend the winter without blackouts.

Ultimately, Kateryna left with her son for Croatia: "There is power here and no curfew, but we still don't go outside after sunset. We live by the sea, which we had only dreamed about before, but we don't notice it because we are constantly reading the news. We're here alone. We are strangers here."

Of course, Kateryna feels better about her young son abroad. They are safe there. However, she really wants to go home and is already planning their return in April.

"Children shouldn't live in fear." Tetiana left Kharkiv with her children

On 24 February 2022, Tetiana woke up to the sound of explosions and immediately thought, "Oh my God, has it really started?" For the previous few days, all she could talk to her friends and family about was the possibility of Russia attacking Ukraine. But it was still hard for Tetiana to believe such savagery could happen in the 21st century.

She went into her living room to find her husband already awake. Soon, the whole street had woken up. There were non-stop phone calls and messages. Everyone was in shock. Tetiana didn't know what to do, even though she had been packing her emergency bag for over a week. Her husband insisted on it.

Tetiana's husband decided to go to work and to play things by ear. Tetiana was scared to death, so he took her and their children to her mother's house on the next street. Her house at least had a good basement, which provided a sort of illusion of safety.

On 1 March, Kharkiv was constantly bombed, and Tetiana's family stayed in the basement all day. In the evening, a missile strike wiped out a house nearby.

> "I have never experienced such horror in my life! The basement was shaking, the top door was open, and it was incredibly loud. I thought it was the end," Tetiana recalls.

The family stayed in the basement that night, though neither Tetiana nor her husband got any sleep.

In the morning, right after curfew lifted, Tetiana and her husband got into their car and drove home to get their belongings. Then they returned for their kids and left Kharkiv. Tetiana's husband's parents and her mother refused to evacuate.

The trip from Kharkiv was very long. It took the family a week to reach the Polish border.

They first drove 8 hours to Poltava, which would normally take just two hours. The traffic on the road was crazy, as many people had decided to leave that day. The family spent the night in Poltava and set off again in the morning, although they did not know where they were ultimately headed.

A day later, they arrived in Haisyn, Vinnytsia Oblast, where they had booked an apartment, but the owner of the apartment took their advance payment and disappeared. As a result, the family spent the whole day in a café because they had nowhere else to go.

In the evening, a wonderfully generous woman gave them shelter at her home for free. Tetiana's family spent a few days there and then moved on again. The family's next stop was Kropyvnytskyi, and on 8 March they reached Chervonohrad, Lviv Oblast, where they spent the night in a hotel.

The next morning, Tetiana and her children crossed the Polish border. "It was a difficult but right decision. Children shouldn't live in fear!" Tetiana says.

After numerous relocations, searching for housing, and working with various volunteers, Tetiana and her children settled in France. Like all Ukrainians, they dream of victory and peace in their homeland.

Meeting empathy and help in Poland. Nadiia from Kyiv was evacuated to Poland with her children

My two small children and I were passengers on an evacuation train. It was terrible, dark, and cold. But we were lucky: there were so many scared people, but my children had their own bunk (an incredible luxury). I was riding on a folding seat and thanked God because my friend and her mother rode on the floor.

I remember Mariia, a girl whose house was hit by a rocket. Seeing that I was already at the end of my strength, she took care of my children on the way. Kostyk still remembers her and wants to see her again. I thank her to the moon and back.

Children were collected from several compartments, 6-7 of them, and any of the adults who could go to entertain them. Others were sobbing at this time. They cried, wiped off their snot, and went to play with the children.

A woman who evacuated with a hamster brought it for the children to pet. The woman who left with the French bulldog also brought him to be petted by the children. It was like a petting zoo.

To the Poles: how can we repay this debt? At our first stop, they brought food from some restaurant. Each box has the inscription "Hold on, brothers!" I was very impressed by this. At the second stop: a crowd of Poles threw baby food, diapers, wet wipes, and toys through the windows.

For some reason, I was especially impressed by a woman with a large package of pads, who generously handed them over. It was so needed. People with posters, people who just came to wave at us, crying.

Warsaw railway station. A child my daughter's age hands out bags of bananas, candy, yogurt, and tissues. Volunteers are God's vicars on Earth. A woman boiled soup and poured it into jars. My children ate hot food for the first time in two days.

A woman named Liuda told us, "I didn't bring anything, but I've been here for a long time, I know Polish, I will translate for you, and I will look after the children." Poles are a crazy organization, like an anthill. Even the policemen entertained the children.

The bus drivers in Toruń let us and the children stay at the depot at night so that we could wait for our journey in warmth and with a toilet. They cried and showed pictures of their children, who were just as young as ours.

We were going to an apartment, and the driver asked: "Is it true that there is another train with 800 people? You don't know? Well, I'll go back to the station and wait anyway. Why? Because I have to."

Nadiia and her children have since returned home to Kyiv. She is very grateful to the Polish people for their sensitivity and kind hearts.

"My cat is my hero." Nataliia managed to evacuate from Mariupol with her old cat Marta. She tells her story

My cat Marta, a Scottish Fold, is already 16. What has she not yet experienced, and now a war! A real war in Mariupol. It was 56 days of hell in our apartment. Practically alone.

My cat is my hero. When the invasion began, she, like all of us, did not yet fully understand what had happened. Apparently, her cat did not believe it until the end. Like us, she had no idea what to expect.

Endless and terrible stress was waiting for her. Especially in the evenings. A constant glow and roar. Strong, haunting, and murderous. Horror. But I'm sure she was most annoyed by our panic and running around. We were disturbing her sacred peace and comfort.

Just imagine: she has just settled down to sleep next to me, and here we (me, my husband, and my son) are already quickly running away somewhere.

We knew we were running to hide. Marta did not understand the seriousness of the danger and the proximity of death. We saw the houses burning, but she didn't. We saw pockets of fire spreading from each explosion. She didn't. She just slept and was woken up.

Marta did not run like us to hide first in the corridor, and then in the basement. She just watched. In a cat's way. I think my cat was feeling stressed in her own way. But she definitely felt it. I saw it in her eyes.

After March 10, when a new era of our family's survival began, she became completely perplexed. On this day, right before our eyes, an enemy strike destroyed four apartments in the building across from us. And when the smoke cleared and the dust settled, we ran to the basement in order to hide there. But without Marta...

Did she then realize that she could die? From shelling. Or hunger. Or loneliness.

Visiting Marta three times a day became my new ritual. I had to feed her, kiss her, and put warm things near her because it was cold. I kept whispering to her that I would never leave her and that everything would be fine. I tried to calm Marta down and calm myself around her.

And she persevered. She got out of that hell with us. The evacuation was very stressful and lasted 29 hours from Mariupol to Zaporizhzhia. All this time my dear cat was lying on my lap. She did not sleep at all, as it was very scary. For all of us. We were terrified by the uncertainty, Grad rocket explosions near our buses, and snipers along the roadside.

But we got out! We were saved. We endured it all. In one report about those who "escaped from hell," my Marta is there in a photo. My 16-year-old fearless, wise, and thoughtful cat. My hero!

The occupiers' furious faces. The story of deacon Mykola, whose family escaped Russian occupation

Mykola Serdiuk is a deacon at the village of Havrylivka, Kyiv Oblast. In February 2022, he understood that a full-scale war was possible, but he refused to believe it would actually happen. On Monday, February 21, he had a brotherhood meeting to discuss what they needed to do during wartime, and what to do during bombing raids, when there was no power supply. Mykola listened to these instructions but did not think that he would really need them.

And yet full-scale war did come to Ukraine. On February 24, Mykola's daughter called and told him that fires were raging in Kharkiv and Vasylkiv. Mykola, who worked in Kyiv, moved from the capital to the village with his family, believing it would be safer there.

"When we were leaving, I saw many cars heading in the opposite direction: from Liutizh to Kyiv. I also thought: why are we leaving when people are coming in? Apparently, the people knew that it would be safer in Kyiv because the capital is better protected by the army," Mykola recalls.

Mykola planned to leave his wife and grandson in the village and return to Kyiv. However, when he reached the village, he learned that the bridges in Hostomel and Demydiv had already been blown up and he could no longer return to the capital.

On February 24, the first Russian equipment advanced into Ukraine. It was reported on the radio that they had broken across the border. The Russians pushed through Ivankiv, captured the Chornobyl nuclear power plant, and advanced onwards. Mykola heard the Russian troops approaching.

He later learned that the Russians had landed at the Hostomel airfield. The enemy captured the airfield and heavy shelling began. It was scary because it was so nearby – just 12–13 km from Havrylivka.

On February 25, the power went out in the village because the lines had been cut somewhere. On February 26, intense explosions became more frequent. Mykola realized that the Russians were shelling Bucha, Irpin, and Hostomel. A lot of Russian equipment passed through Havrylivka and the village was occupied. The Russians ordered the residents to remain at home and not venture outside. If anyone had to go outside, they were instructed to wear white armbands.

When the windows in Mykola's apartment were shattered by shelling, the family gathered their essential belongings and ran to hide in the basement of the local school. However, there was no room for them, either there or in the basement of the kindergarten. In the end, the family found shelter in the basement of a grocery store. The shelling was extremely heavy, with explosions heard every 2–3 minutes.

On March 8, the gas supply in the village was also cut off. People began to carry firewood, take out fireplaces, and light fires to warm themselves and cook food.

Mykola said that Havrylivka was occupied by Chechen, Russian, and Belarusian soldiers. Mykola once asked one of them why they had come, especially seeing that no one had a gas and power supply, heat, or food. The occupier answered him with sarcasm, "It wasn't us. It was your own Ukrainians who bombed you." Mykola told the Russian soldiers to return to where they had come from and said that the Ukrainians did not need to be liberated from anything. He saw the occupiers' furious faces and fell silent. He turned around and left. Fortunately, the Russian soldiers did not do anything to him.

In the meantime, the Russians occupied dachas in the forest and lived very well in them. Those houses had fireplaces and there was plenty of food. Mykola learned that Ukrainian troops would soon launch an offensive. The Russian invaders began to hide in the houses of local residents. Mykola realized he needed to leave as soon as possible because an intense battle was sure to come right there in his own village.

People began to leave by car, while others walked in a large column with white armbands. Mykola gathered his entire family and took a gamble on leaving, despite rumors that the Russians were not letting people go and were even shooting some of them.

Mykola asked everyone to pray and get into the car. An armored personnel carrier and four Russian soldiers were on guard at the first checkpoint. They carefully inspected the family, but let them through. Mykola drove through the village from where the Russians were firing upon Bucha. There were many tanks and all manner of military equipment. Mykola's family passed the second and third checkpoints with their hands raised and praying aloud.

At the last checkpoint, the occupiers stopped Mykola's car. He came out with his hands raised and asked in Russian if they would let his family through. The soldiers asked if Mykola had any cigarettes. He replied that his family is religious, so they did not smoke. Fortunately, the Russians let Mykola go.

During the next 2-3 km of the road, Mykola counted 20 Russian tanks in the fields. Some soldiers were standing around smoking, others were sitting on tanks with weapons in their hands. Then he saw destroyed cars of civilians and dead bodies, dusted with snow. Everyone was terrified by the sight.

Mykola and his family finally reached Makariv, where there already were Ukrainian soldiers and blue and yellow flags. It was a joyous sight.

At three o'clock the following morning, the family reached Yavoriv, Lviv Oblast, where volunteers were waiting for them. Mykola and his family were brought to a school, fed, and allowed to sleep and rest. Then they found a house nearby, where they settled temporarily.

The family felt they could finally relax, but on the very first night of their stay, the Russians hit the Yavoriv military base with four missiles. Mykola hadn't heard such powerful explosions even when he was under Russian occupation. The windows in the houses were blown out and everything shook. "We had fled our homes, but the war followed us here," Mykola said.

His family has since returned home. Mykola says that his outlook has changed and he has begun to value life, people, and his ministry even more.

This text is based on testimony collected by the Kharkiv Human Rights Protection Group.

"People were knocking on the train door, begging to be let on." Valentyna tells a story of her journey from Russian-shelled Kramatorsk

Valentyna Bondarenko had been familiar with war since 2014 when hostilities began in eastern Ukraine. It was then that she learned what missiles, Grad rockets, and automatic gunfire sounded like. She suffered a stroke as a result of these events.

In February 2022, war returned to Kramatorsk once more. On the day of the full-scale invasion, Valentyna's neighbors gathered at the front entrance to discuss their course of action.

Since Valentyna and her husband had nowhere to go, they began to furnish a nearby basement. Young men helped to clean the area and put up bunks. In the dust and cold, Valentyna and her husband had to sleep on these bunks during the shelling of the city. They were forced to run several times a day from their apartment on the fourth floor to the basement.

Almost all shops in Kramatorsk quickly shut down. Only one store selling bread and sugar remained open in the House of Trade. Valentyna stocked up on meat in advance, so she and her husband would have enough to eat until they had to leave the city.

Little by little, people began to leave Kramatorsk, and there was almost no one on the streets. It reached a point when Valentyna, feeling alone and frightened, convinced her husband they had to leave.

> "We took some items and clothes and went out onto the street. We saw a car in the distance, near the basement and I shouted for it to stop. The driver was reluctant because of the sirens, but eventually agreed to take us to the station," Valentyna recalls of her departure.

There was a huge crowd of people at the station. Valentyna and her husband did not care which train they boarded, as they had no relatives or acquaintances to stay with anywhere else. When it started to get dark, the air-raid siren sounded and people rushed to hide as quickly as possible in the station building. "The crowd nearly crushed us! I had dropped my bags and thought I'd never survive," Valentyna explained.

Later, a volunteer took Valentyna and her husband to board a train. People entered the carriages and turned on their flashlights. The train traveled in the dark and, for safety reasons, it was forbidden to turn on the lights. The journey was slow with occasional, protracted stops in what appeared to be the middle of fields.

When the overcrowded train stopped in Lozova, people started knocking on the door, begging to be let on. There were families with children and, although there were very few seats on the train, these people were evacuated. They related that they had been hiding from bombing raids and, seeing the train, they had made a run for it and tried to stop it.

Valentyna said that the Russians had shelled Kramatorsk every day, striking factories, schools, and a hospital. "I think they destroyed the entire infrastructure and it seems there is nothing left to target. They have now started searching the villages around the city," she said.

One of Valentyna's acquaintances from Kramatorsk witnessed a terrible incident when a small girl's head was blown off as she was walking with her mother. Valentyna says a similar incident occurred in 2014, when two men were walking from their garages. These are the awful realities of the Russian invasion.

As a result of the bombing, there is now a huge crater near Valentyna's house. She doesn't know what has happened to her home and is not sure if she will have anywhere to return to after victory.

This text is based on testimony collected by the Kharkiv Human Rights Protection Group.

"People were buried in public squares, parks, and next to their houses." Vira survived the apocalypse in Mariupol

Vira Tiata worked as a teacher in a kindergarten in Mariupol her whole life. After the full-scale Russian invasion on February 24, she was forced to flee the city. She later learned that her house had been destroyed.

Heavy shelling in Mariupol began on March 4. Vira and her neighbor hid in the bathroom, covering themselves with pillows. Then cars started burning under her house, windows were blown out in apartments, and Vira's first-floor neighbors were killed.

Sometimes Vira and her neighbor Tania also hid in the basement of a nearby store. One day, the area where Vira lived was bombarded by the Russians with Grad rockets. The windows on Vira's balcony were damaged. At that moment, she and her neighbor were hiding in the bathroom. After that, they decided to go to the bomb shelter at the school nearby.

Even though the conditions there were poor, and people had to cook food on bricks, Vira still felt a little safer.

"We cooked porridge and pasta. Once the bombing ended, men ran to the school nurse's office, carrying chairs, school desks, and anything they could to sit on. Mattresses were brought from the kindergarten. I took a blanket from home, and my neighbor brought some provisions and a sleeping bag. That's how she and I lived on the chairs. Volunteers brought us water and food," Vira recalls.

Vira tried not to leave the shelter because the bombing outside was so intense that the windows shook. She spent 12 days in the school's basement. Then her children who lived in another district of Mariupol came to get her and convinced her to leave the city.

> "The bombings were terrible, the explosions were terrible. Cars were on fire and buildings were all turned black. Our building was all black: burned down and bombed out. The windows and doors were all blown out. The balcony was destroyed and collapsed," Vira said.

"I left everything we had earned since 1963. Everything we had... I had bought a new refrigerator for the kitchen. My husband and

I worked. We bought a stove, and new windows. We built a new balcony. All this has been destroyed."

Leaving Mariupol was not easy. A huge line of cars had gathered. people were driving broken-down cars, with broken, shot-through windows. Instead of 20 minutes, Vira and her children waited for 6 hours to leave the city. After that, the road was a little less busy. The cars began going their separate ways.

Vira remembers how Russian soldiers took away a man's car at a checkpoint. They ordered him to step out and show his documents, then pushed him aside and took his car away. Also, during the evacuation, Vira saw a husband and wife come under enemy fire: the man's hands and his wife's legs were blown off.

In the end, Vira and her children came to Ananiiv, Odesa Oblast. Vira's brother lives in Russia. And although it was closer to go there, the family could not ask for help from the country which had so brutally attacked them.

"You know, I really want to go to my hometown. But people who came from there later say that the city is completely destroyed. So many people were buried... People were first buried in public squares: civilians whose houses were destroyed. And then people began to be buried in parks. Later, there was no place to bury them, so people were buried just next to their houses," Vira said.

Vira's neighbors who left later say that they saw many crosses on the streets. In the summer, terribly unsanitary conditions emerged in Mariupol. Although the Russian occupiers have announced that the water supply will be restored, it is yet to come back. Everything is destroyed, and all the pipes are broken.

Vira's younger son, with whom she ran away from Mariupol, lives in Ukraine, and the older one lives in Russia. She loves them both equally, but because of their different attitudes to the war, they do not communicate. Vira is very hurt by this, as well as by the fact that her hometown and home have been destroyed. She doesn't understand why Russia attacked Ukraine and cannot talk about the war without tears.

This text is based on testimony collected by the Kharkiv Human Rights Protection Group.

Shattered Homes: Stories of Ruin Amidst Russian Bombing

Russian missiles destroy apartments, but not the lust for life. Ania from Kyiv lost her home to Russian shelling and tells her story

February 22. We decided to go to our hometown of Sumy to visit our parents. I told my husband to take our documents. We were planning to be gone for just three days, so all we had was the things that were on us.

February 24. I woke up at 5 am to my husband telling me, "that's it, the war has begun." Complete confusion about what to do next. We didn't have a car, so we took tickets to Kyiv. Outside the window, there was already a kilometer-long queue for fuel.

Sirens in the city were not working yet, and Telegram channels for air raids had not yet been created. The only source of information is the news, which is played non-stop on all TV channels. They only talk about Sumy. Enemy vehicles are already moving in a column through the center of the city.

Mark, my son, is very quiet. He almost does not speak and does not want to eat. First sleepless night. The whole building was shaking. We heard explosions and the rumble of equipment.

February 25. The railway connection with Sumy is suspended. The city is surrounded by Russian checkpoints, and no one is allowed out. There is a feeling of being in a "mouse trap" and complete despair.

I thank my husband for making the decision to leave and his family for giving up their car and saying "try to save yourself." In 5 minutes we were in the car with the feeling that we were saying goodbye forever. It was possible to leave the city on country roads. The scariest part was getting on the highway.

On one side, a Russian checkpoint on the way out of the city, which we bypassed; on the other side, a column of enemy vehicles headed for Kyiv. We had to drive 5 minutes to the exit from the highway, so we drove along this column.

I closed my eyes, the child was silent, and my husband hit the gas. We drove by. We had to reach the right-bank Ukraine and then decide what to do next.

February 26. Night. Somewhere near Cherkasy, we ran over a hole in the road and punctured a wheel. Suddenly, a man ran out of nowhere and started shouting that we were being bombed. My heart was racing, my hands were shaking, but in 4 minutes we changed the tire.

We arrived in Bila Tserkva at 2 am. We wanted to spend the night there, but there was nowhere available. We even asked to stay in the hospital, but we were not allowed.

We drove further towards Vinnytsia. 48 hours in panic and without sleep took their toll, and hallucinations began. We stopped in the town of Pohrebyshche, where a kind woman gave us shelter.

We were taken to a room where we could sleep a little. Mark went to the toilet for the first time in 20 hours, and that was with persuasion.

February 27. At night, we reached Ternopil, where my husband's colleagues took us in. We were able to take a shower and eat breakfast. In this city, we heard sirens for the first time. Next, we went to Volyn, where accommodation awaited us.

February 28 – March 10. Mark calmed down and began to talk little by little. We all got sick: cough, fever, nausea, upset stomachs. All symptoms that the body has experienced stress.

March 11. This night I could not sleep because I felt something bad was about to happen. At 5:47, without any warning, ballistic missiles landed. 4 of them. This picture, seen with my own eyes, will remain with me forever.

I pushed my husband, grabbed my child, and ran out into the corridor. Then planes flew by, and everything was shaking and terrifying. The next day we moved to another apartment because I could not even go to the window anymore.

April 28. We spent the day with new friends. In the evening, the air alarm started, and we went to hide in the shelter. At 8:16 pm, messages began to arrive from the chat room of our building in Kyiv: a Russian missile had hit it.

We saw the first photos in the news and realized that our apartment was at the epicenter of the explosion. After that, something changed inside me.

You know, it's kind of strange to look at the ruins of your home and think "it's not all that bad." We have accepted this fact as much as possible. Thank God that we had been far away, and that now we are together and have not lost the ability to enjoy life despite everything.

I sincerely believe in myself, in our family, that everything will be much better. We did it once, we will do it again! The only thing I dream about is basic security, which was taken away from everyone who decided to stay in Ukraine.

"Son, they are bombing us!" The story of Mykola, who survived the horrific assault on Kharkiv

Until February 23, Mykola had been working with his son as a handyman repairing apartments. On February 24, he woke up, not understanding what was going on. He heard some kind of explosions or thunder.

Suddenly, the first missiles struck military facilities. The Russians hit the Kharkiv tank school, struck the cadet corps, and destroyed the city's main bazaar. Then their bombs hit a residential building and damaged a supermarket. The Russians also destroyed a building of the city's detention center. Mykola does not know how many inmates were there. Then more powerful bombing began. Mykola said that the Russian military bombarded the city in a way that it is hard to describe. "I don't remember what date, at ten in the morning I talked to my son on the phone. I heard fighter jets buzzing over the house. I shout: "Son, they are bombing us!"

A missile passed almost over the house and aimed at homes near the railway station. The explosion was so powerful that Mykola's house shook. Black smoke was visible on the street, and ash descended into Mykola's yard.

One day, Mykola recalls, an aerial bomb landed on the city's central square. There was a volunteer tent, and the bomb hit it. "And what's left of Saltivka... The Russians destroyed almost the entire neighborhood."

> "A lot of people died. One girl was walking with blood on her leg. People were standing in line for food, and a shell hit nearby. The old lady's leg was torn off, and blood splattered on the girl. The girl was shocked. She was 15-16 years old," – Mykola recalled.

The regions of Oleksiivka and Piatykhatky suffered a great deal. There are no military facilities there, only residential buildings. Mykola said that before the war, there were good roads in Kharkiv, and Gorky Park was like Disneyland. "Everything that could be destroyed was destroyed."

Mykola has a cousin who lives in Arkhangelsk, Russia. She told him that he is a Banderite, and that Bandera's people killed her grandfather. Mykola asked: "Have you ever met these Bandera people? Do you even understand who Bandera is? The man has been gone for many years, and you are still afraid of him. You are crazy over there!" But it was useless to try to prove anything to her, as many Russians are brainwashed. Mykola doesn't speak to his cousin anymore. "I really want everything they (the Russians) have done to be returned to them. And I don't want anything else."

This text is based on testimony collected by the Kharkiv Human Rights Protection Group.

"We don't have an apartment anymore." Kateryna lost her home in Kharkiv after a Russian strike

Until February 24, 21-year-old Kateryna Hurina had been studying hard to complete her bachelor's degree while working as a graphic designer at a real estate agency. She lived with her parents and pet dog in Pivnichna Saltivka, a district of Kharkiv on the outskirts of the city, where she had spent most of her life.

Kateryna loved her district very much. "There were always many families out with their children and walking their dogs. I liked living away from the center; it was like we had our own little town inside a big city," she says.

During the night from 23 to 24 February, Kateryna had a dream about war, but when she awoke the next morning, war had become a reality. Car alarms were blaring, lights were flashing, and explosions filled the air. "I went into the kitchen and my parents were looking out the window. It reminded me of the scene from the TV series Chernobyl, when people stood on the bridge, watching the burning reactor. We didn't know what to do," Kateryna recalls.

Kateryna's family decided that the safest place in their apartment was the bathroom, so that is where they hid during the shelling. Most of their neighbors had gone down to the basement, but it was very cold there. It had not been designed to be a bomb shelter and there was not enough space.

On the second day of the full-scale invasion, the Russians hit the building where Kateryna's classmate lived, the apartment of her father's friend, and then a high-rise building on their street.

On March 1, Kateryna's parents went to the shop, leaving her alone with her dog in the bathroom. She heard an incredibly loud explosion and, as she sat on the floor, she thought that her life was about to end.

Her friend called her, saying, "Katya, your house is on fire!" A missile had hit the nearby entrance, on the seventh or eighth floor. That day, Kateryna and her parents thought a lot about evacuating but they could not bring themselves to do so. They thought that a second strike wouldn't come. But it did.

On March 4, the Russians shelled Pivnichna Saltivka mercilessly. Kateryna's mother was working at the grocery store and standing at the cash register when a missile struck. It killed a man standing nearby, crushing him in an instant. Kateryna's mother hid under the counter and had to crouch beside the dead man, waiting for the shelling to end. Then she ran home, amid burning houses, downed communications lines, and dead bodies.

It was then that the family decided to leave Kharkiv and they went to Kateryna's grandparents in Liubotyn, Kharkiv Oblast.

> "I was happy to be leaving the shelling, but my sense of security didn't last long. On the evening of March 9, when everyone was sleeping, I heard the sound of aircraft. I picked up my dog and ran out into the corridor, screaming to wake the family. At that moment, I heard a very loud explosion, everything shook and the windows were blown out," Kateryna recalls.

When Kateryna's father went out to check what had happened, he saw two rockets land in the yard, a meter from the wall, next to where Kateryna had been standing at the time of the explosion. After that, Kateryna was in a terrible emotional state, having terrible dreams and suffering bouts of depression. It was then that her parents advised her to leave the country. Kateryna left, but her parents remained in Liubotyn.

Meanwhile, Russia continued to bomb Kharkiv. On the night of April 9–10, a rocket completely destroyed Kateryna's apartment. She had already made it safely out of the country when her mother sent her a video taken by a passer-by with the words, "That's it, Katya, we don't have an apartment anymore."

After the launch of the full-scale invasion, Kateryna radically changed her attitude towards Russians. "When the war started in the East of Ukraine and Crimea was occupied, I was 13 years old. Then I thought that it was all Putin and that there were sensible people there among the Russians. I even had three friends from there. However, when the shell hit my house on March 1, they didn't write anything to me, even though they had seen posts about it on social media. It was then that I realized there is no such thing as a good Russian; they are all responsible. Unfortunately, I needed a missile to destroy my home to understand this," Kateryna says.

This text is based on testimony collected by the Kharkiv Human Rights Protection Group.

"The Russians 'liberated' me from my own house."
The story of Ihor from Moshchun

35-year-old Ihor had been living in Moshchun for 8 years, along with his wife, two children, and grandfather. He worked in construction and traveled to work in Kyiv and Irpin.

"We didn't think there would be a war. It was only when we heard the explosions on the 24th that we realized the full extent of the situation. We were hoping the Russians wouldn't come here. On the 24th, when it all started, many people came back to us from Kyiv. We thought it was safer here, but it actually proved to be more dangerous," Ihor recalls.

The sight of Russian helicopters on February 24 was terrifying for Ihor's family. He counted about 56 of them, flying very low over the houses. They were flying to Hostomel to bomb the airport. Ihor also saw two SU fighters flying over Hostomel and Bucha. At first, he thought they were Ukrainian planes, but he later heard from his cousin that they were Russian and that the family had to flee.

On February 26, the house of Ihor's uncle Mykola was burned down. It had most likely been struck by an infantry fighting vehicle. Since the house was made of wood, it caught fire immediately. That day, many roofs were shot through, and there was a large column of smoke in the field from a missile strike.

On February 28, Ihor took his wife, children, and grandfather to the Pushcha-Vodytsia school bomb shelter. He returned to buy cigarettes for the Ukrainian soldiers who had asked him. That same day, three houses burned in Moshchun and there was heavy gunfire and shelling.

On March 3, the Ukrainian military asked all the residents of the village to evacuate quickly, because "there would be hell." Ihor and his family went to the Khmelnytskyi Oblast.

On April 14, Ihor returned home by himself, because he'd heard about looting in the village and wanted to make sure his own house remained unscathed. Once he arrived, he spent a few days at home and hid all the remaining valuables. Ihor realized that Russian soldiers had been in his yard and basement. He found Russian bulletproof vests and other equipment. The Russians had stolen Ihor's electric bike and charger, as well as his power supply unit. They had also stolen a lot from Ihor's neighbors.

Ihor's house had been damaged by artillery shelling, causing the walls and roof to collapse. Since Ihor is a professional builder, he plans to rebuild the house himself.

Ihor's children and wife returned to Moshchun in May and, since then, the family has been living at home. They lived the first few days with a neighbor whose house was in better shape. Once they had cleaned and fixed things, they returned to their own home.

Ihor says that about 80% of the houses in Moshchun had been destroyed. Russian soldiers had killed many people.

> "There was a grandpa here, Oleksii… He stayed and he died. Or he was killed; nobody knows for sure. He used to walk around here, and no one had time to come and pick him up," Ihor explains.

Ihor also said that the houses where the Russians had lived remained intact. At Ihor's friends' house, they'd left a terrible mess behind, and used the bath as a toilet. The Russians had even slaughtered a pig in the house of one of Ihor's neighbors. When the neighbor returned home after the village had been liberated, there were puddles of blood everywhere and the pig's head and skin had been left on the floor.

After the full-scale invasion, Ihor's attitude towards the Russians changed drastically. "They thought that our life was worse than theirs? On the contrary: when they came here, they saw that everyone had their own house, and that we were orderly. My attitude towards them is this: if I see one – I'll knock them out. Because they're bastards given what they've done, 'liberating' us… From what have you liberated us? The house that you've destroyed?"

This text is based on testimony collected by documenters of the Kharkiv Human Rights Group.

A shell flew into the room, knocking out the wall and the window. Hanna's apartment in Horenka was hit by Russian bombing

Hanna had a feeling that there would be a big war. There was talk about it on social networks and in the news. Everyone knew that there was a concentration of Russian troops on the border. And then foreign embassy staff started leaving Ukraine.

Hanna's family had stocked up on food for the New Year. She decided that if they did not need this food, she would give it away.

On February 24, Hanna was set to go to work, but at 5 a.m. her daughter woke her up and said: "Mom, it's started!" The family had talked about the possibility of war in advance, so they even had a plan for where and how to hide in the forest. Of course adrenaline was running high that day. Hanna felt both stress and readiness to act:

> *"We all knew what things we were taking. One backpack and that's it. Whole lives packed into single backpacks. I don't know how to put into words that pain and despair. We remained at home until the next day. We gave the Ukrainian soldiers tea because it was very cold."*

The first day was difficult, as people were streaming out of Kyiv for almost the whole day, and there were heavy traffic jams. There were a lot of cars, and people took their dogs and cats. But many people still remained in Horenka. On the night of March 3–4, when the heavy bombardment began, Ukrainian soldiers came and told people that the area would soon turn very hot. Then people started leaving en masse.

Hanna's family first went to Pushcha-Vodytsia, but this area would soon also come under Russian shelling. So the family went to their friend in Kropyvnytskyi. They stayed there for a month, and on April 7, Hanna and her husband returned home.

There was no electricity or gas when they arrived. Since Hanna's house was on the frontline, there were a lot of destroyed buildings around.

On the night of March 7–8, a bomb was dropped on Hanna's apartment building. The people who were in the building at that time were covered with dust and debris. But within a day, they found a way out and left. All of the eight people survived. Fortunately, save for the windows and doors, Hanna's apartment survived.

"We have two apartments here," Hanna said, "We lived in one apartment, and we were renovating the other. We were supposed to move in May. We had to take my husband's mother, since she is disabled. Now it is possible to live in one apartment, but not in the other. A shell flew into the room there, knocking out the wall and the window."

Hanna is now trying to keep living and encourage other people: "I knew that we would return here. That we would not go abroad. It may sound presumptuous, but I knew I needed to be here. I am not alone: my husband, my children, and the church are with me. We are trying to help people. We bring humanitarian aid, food, drinking water, and we prepare food. We are needed here."

This text is based on testimony collected by the Kharkiv Human Rights Protection Group.

"I left my home in my trousers, boots, and a jacket."
The story of Petro from Moschun

Petro Neshchadym is 62 years old. He and his family had lived in Moschun, Kyiv Oblast for the past 15 years. He has moved to Cherkasy, as his house was completely destroyed during the hostilities.

On February 24, Petro was finishing his shift at work and did not really believe that the full-scale war would begin. However, when 28 Russian helicopters flew over his house in Moshchun, he got really scared. Petro saw these helicopters circling over the Hostomel airfield and firing. He had previously served in aviation himself and saw that they were flying very low, about a meter from the tops of the trees.

Petro also saw Russian soldiers storming Hostomel. Their landing lasted for about 20 minutes, after which a shootout ensued. Later, the helicopters departed.

During the following days, there was continuous shelling. Petro's daughter and grandchildren were evacuated immediately, while he and his wife remained in Moschun until March 6. One day, Petro's house was hit by an enemy shell, leaving everything blown apart and on fire. He managed to put the fire out himself but, once he'd left Moshchun, his house was destroyed.

At first, many people remained in Moschun. The local residents hoped that all this would not last long. However, when Ukrainian troops drove a lot of equipment into the village and asked the residents to evacuate, the majority did so.

Petro says that he was left without any property due to the Russian invasion: "I evacuated in the trousers, boots, and jacket I was wearing, with nothing but my documents." Everything else he owned that had remained in Moschun had been either looted or destroyed as a result of shelling.

> "The Russians smashed through the front door of my house with an ax, shot out my neighbor's lock, stole all the clothes of my other neighbors, took women's shoes and anything they could get their hands on. Literally every house was broken into," Petro explains.

The main thing for Petro, of course, is that he and his relatives are alive. He knows that his neighbor's mother was very badly wounded in the head and neck and ended up hanging herself. Petro also heard many stories about the dead and missing residents of Moschun.

Petro is now waiting for the war to end as soon as possible. Since he is a builder by profession, he plans to build a new house after Ukraine's victory. Despite the fact that he and his wife are no longer young and do not earn that much, he has not lost hope for the best and believes that he will be able to start everything from scratch.

This text is based on testimony collected by the Kharkiv Human Rights Protection Group.

"Dogs were pulling at human remains." The story of Ninelle from Borodianka

On the first day of Russia's full-scale invasion, Ninelle was not afraid. She, like other residents of Borodianka, believed that everything would be fine and she did not want to leave her home.

However, on March 1, she saw Russian military equipment driving down her street. Ninelle and her family did not spend that night at home, but when she returned the next day, she witnessed real horror: smashed windows and doors, a completely devastated street, and corpses of people lying all around.

Ninelle did not know where to step or how to enter her own apartment, but she and her family mustered their strength and took everything they could from their home. No one from Ninelle's apartment complex was killed, although there were many casualties from the neighboring building, which had been bombed. The street was littered with corpses, arms, legs, and heads. Dogs were pulling at human remains.

> "What was strange was that all the bombs that the Russians dropped on Borodianka were so accurate that there are no craters anywhere near the houses; they were all direct hits," Ninelle explained.

In the first days of the war, she explained, the Russians shot at any people they happened to spot.

"I heard that Russian soldiers came to the house where a family lived. They told the father that they wanted his wife and they took her away. When he began protesting, he was shot in front of his family. Then the Russians shot two of their own soldiers so that they wouldn't tell anyone about what had happened."

Ninelle also remembered the story of how Russian invaders brazenly took a house on the outskirts of Borodianka. To control the crossing, they just went in and shot the whole family that lived there.

"They were looking around for Nazis. They found none so they just killed ordinary people instead," Ninelle said.

While Ninelle's family could not leave Borodianka, they simply prayed and watched as bombs fell on the neighboring houses. In those moments, Ninelle's house would shake and several times she resigned herself to her death.

Fortunately, Ninelle and her family managed to escape. However, after returning home, she found her apartment completely destroyed, her car damaged beyond repair, and her garage demolished. Her family was left with absolutely nothing. That said, Ninelle is glad that at least they are alive.

"We'll rebuild everything. We'll be fine. And our military will drive out all our enemies. I always knew that victory would be ours, Crimea would be ours, and everything would be ours again. I simply could not believe, however, that it would come at such a price," Ninelle admits.

This text is based on testimony collected by documenters of the Kharkiv Human Rights Group.

Torment and Humiliation: Enduring Russian Brutality

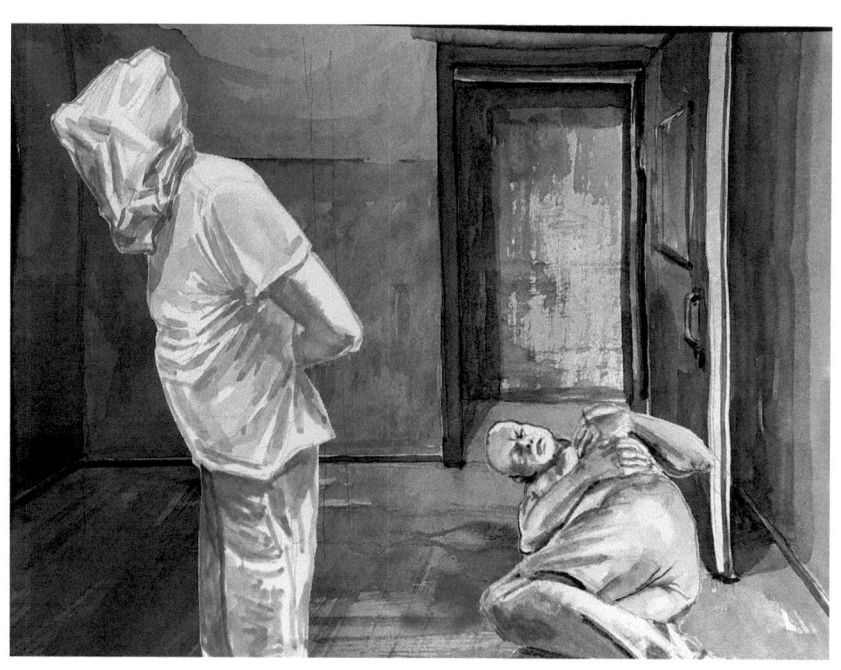

The Russians would come to your home at 5 a.m.
Viktoriia describes searches in Russian-occupied Kherson

Viktoriia Kirilova survived the 8-month occupation of Kherson. She describes how Russians searched people's homes and took people for interrogation.

Home searches could be divided into two types, she says.

1. Between 9 and 12 armed officers would enter a home. Sometimes they would say they were from the Security Service of Ukraine (SBU) because they were driving cars with Ukrainian license plates stolen from local residents. Of course, they could not have been from the SBU, because the occupiers would have imprisoned or shot any SBU personnel they could get their hands on.

If you were lucky, the hours-long interrogation would take place at your home, Viktoriia says. The occupiers would pressure people to collaborate with them and to sign cooperation papers.

If you were unlucky, you were taken out with a bag over your head and disappeared. The fate of many people taken like this remains unknown. Despite the joy of being liberated on the one hand, many Khersonians still have no idea where their relatives and friends are, or whether they are even alive.

These raids would usually happen at 5-6 am to catch people by surprise. They seized phones, computers, and absolutely everything that they might find of interest.

2. The second type of search was conducted by Russia's FSB or the police from the so-called "Donetsk People's Republic." They would be carried out by 2 or 3 people in civilian clothes with weapons. They were very aggressive and brazen.

Their goal was to extract information about people they could not find. Their visits could happen many times and be violent. They would take people for "conversations," and bring people around to places or properties that they were interested in.

If the person they were looking for had managed to leave Kherson, they searched their home to the last detail and turned everything upside down. After that, the occupiers could settle in the apartment themselves.

Viktoriia said that one of her most important daily tasks was wiping her phone and computer.

"Could I have ever imagined that I would use spyware, hide absolutely all data, set complex passwords everywhere, and have secret chats? I didn't know that my phone could do so many things. I didn't know that I could remember so many passwords. I didn't know that there were so many things to cheat with," Viktoriia explains.

> "You can't go to bed without deleting your browser history, because at night you'll hear your door being kicked in and you won't have time to delete anything from your phone. You can't leave home without a clean phone. You can't have specific apps on your phone, especially Signal, Telegram, or Diia. They will be automatically deleted if they are found during a search. You should always remember that your phone isn't yours. Your phone can determine your fate: whether you will return home today or, at best, you will be taken for interrogation," Viktoriia explained.

Often, young people gave the occupiers old push-button black-and-white phones for inspection. This greatly irritated the Russians and was dangerous, as it could prompt the Russians to search the person more thoroughly.

The Russian invaders came to Viktoriia's home repeatedly and took her for interrogation. They beat her, and she was left with scars both on her body and within.

> "When I was being detained and the occupiers started scaring me that they would take me to the basement, my brain thought of terrible things: 'Well, rape – I can cope with that. Torture – depending on the kind of torture, you start to think about which method is the most painful for you. Murder – I don't want to be killed, I want to live a little longer." These were the thoughts of a free person in the 21st century in an independent state," Viktoriia said.

Unfortunately, this remains the everyday reality for Ukrainians in the regions still occupied by Russia.

Beaten with a heating pipe. Vadym spent 110 days in a Russian torture camp in Kupiansk

Before the full-scale Russian invasion, Vadym Kutsenko served in the Armed Forces, but he had resigned for health reasons before New Year 2022.

In February, he came to Kupiansk to run some errands and it was here that he encountered full-scale war and occupation first-hand. During the occupation, one of the locals reported Vadym to the Russians and he ended up in the infamous temporary detention center at the Kupiansk district police station. According to the Security Service of Ukraine, the Russians illegally detained about 400 Ukrainian citizens in this torture chamber.

On February 24, 2022, Vadym was at a dacha in the village of Hlushkivka near Kupiansk. He was no longer able to leave because the Russians would have detained him as a fugitive at the very first checkpoint. Therefore, he remained in the countryside and planted a vegetable garden. They came for him in May.

Two Russian cars drove up to Vadym's house. The occupiers struck him in the head with a rifle butt and held him face down in the grass. While Vadym lay under the supervision of one of the soldiers, the other six searched the house, kitchen, cellar, attic and outbuildings. They turned everything over, but found nothing. Vadym's hands were bound tightly and he was taken away in an unknown direction.

On the way, the Russians stopped at two more addresses, breaking down the doors with a sledgehammer. They were evidently looking for someone. Throughout this time, Vadym was kept with a bag on his head. His hands were bound with cable ties and they later became very swollen. Dark marks from the ties are still visible on Vadym's wrists.

Vadym was brought to the Kupiansk district police department and placed in one of the cells. Since he had served in the Ukrainian army, he was beaten with a heating pipe, an officer's belt with a buckle, and tortured with electric shocks.

> *"The clamps were attached to me; you can guess where... One clamp on the ear, another – below the stomach. Others were handcuffed from behind. There was a horizontal bar in one of the cells... Some men were beaten so hard that they passed out.*

There was constant swearing and terrible screaming. I have never heard such screams as the ones I heard during the first days of my stay there," Vadym recalls.

Vadym was asked about weapons, why he had served in the Ukrainian army, and whom he knew from there. Of course, he refused to tell them anything.

Vadym was kept in a two-person cell together with eight other men. Some were there simply for breaking the curfew. Some had been there for 10–15 days, and one for an entire month. Vadym spent almost 4 months in the torture chamber.

From time to time, military doctors came to the cells and "resuscitated" those who were already near death. "However, there were times when the occupiers forgot to close the feeding hatches and I saw people being carried out. It was not a box of matches, not something you could take without being noticed. I saw three or four of them dragging a corpse on sheets," said Vadym.

Fortunately, Vadym was tortured only during the first days; the rest of the time he was simply held there in his cell; no one ever answered his question of why he was there. He just sat where he was and listened to new prisoners being interrogated and tortured.

Vadym said the Russians released some of the prisoners but only if they gave interviews calling on Ukrainian soldiers to lay down their arms or cooperate with the enemy. Vadym and many other men could not go against their conscience, so they remained where they were in their cells.

Vadym was released on his 110th day of imprisonment when the Armed Forces of Ukraine had already begun a counteroffensive in Kharkiv Oblast. However, he did not know about this at that point.

"For two days, our feeders were permanently shut. They left us without food or anything else. In the evening of the second day, the prisoners began to knock on the doors. We thought, well, this knocking will result in them beating everyone. It was always like that there: if someone was at fault for something, everyone would be punished. But no one came. We had mostly people of my age in our cell and those who were younger had health problems. The third cell contained regular guys: they dismantled their bunks and started knocking out the bars with them. They probably worked for three hours, all the time occupied with one thought: that the patrol would hear and they would be doomed," Vadym explained.

However, the men managed to force their way out of their cell, find the keys, and open the other cells. Vadym and the other prisoners found their documents and left the district police department. Vadym said that it was not only men being held in the torture chamber, but also women, girls, and anyone from whom the Russians were stealing businesses.

At that time, the Russians were still occupying Kupiansk but, little by little, they had started leaving because of the advance of Ukrainian forces. Vadym and the others were afraid that the Russians would start looking for them, but no one touched them. When Vadym returned to his dacha, the Russians did not even check his documents and they did not care that he had escaped from their torture chamber. They just came armed with automatic weapons and asked for food.

"My friend asked them where they were from and why they had signed up. They said that they were from Omsk or Tomsk and that they wanted to clear their criminal record. They were always emphasizing that the Ukrainians were rich," Vadym said.

This text is based on testimony collected by the Kharkiv Human Rights Protection Group.

Bag on his head, string around his neck.
Vitalii survived Russian torture in Borodianka

On the first day of the war, Vitalii received a call from his mother, who worked as a concierge in Kyiv, and said that she could not leave the capital. Vitalii went to get her, and when they returned around 6 pm, there were already explosions in the Hostomel area. Borodianka itself was still quiet.

In a few days, a great deal of Russian military equipment began driving down the district road and through the center of Borodianka. Then airstrikes began, so Vitalii's wife, mother, and son moved to his father-in-law's place in a nearby village.

Since Vitalii lives in a house, he took people with children from high-rise buildings to his basement. Later, they were evacuated from Borodianka. Vitalii himself remained in the village for the entire occupation.

At first, the Russian occupiers came to Vitalii's home to check the documents. At that time, they did not particularly bother him, only examining the house and telling him to hang a white rag on his house and write "People live here" on the fence.

On March 15, the Russian military came to Vitalii again and began to ask about local partisans, and about where they were getting ammunition. The Russians thoroughly searched Vitalii's house, barn, and basement. They turned everything upside down.

On March 16, he was forcibly taken from his home to an unknown place (the occupiers put a black bag on his head) and kept in a garage for two and a half days. Vitalii was handcuffed and tied to a chair with tape. They terrorized him by firing a gun between his legs and near his ears, as well as kicking him and tasing him. The most frightening thing for Vitalii was when the Russians put a bag on his head and tightened a string around his neck.

After being tortured, the exhausted Vitalii was put in a car and taken back to the village. He was dropped off at a place he knew, so he walked from there in the direction of his home. Of course, it was difficult for Vitalii to move after almost three days tied to a chair in that garage, but he still managed to get home.

On the way, he saw Russian soldiers, either drunk or high, driving around the village on cars and motorcycles, behaving atrociously. When Vitalii came home, he saw that his door, windows, and boiler had been shot through, and the tires on his car were slashed. Then he noticed that the occupiers had stolen his mobile phone, flash drives, bed sheets, and various tools from the garage.

Many people died in Borodianka as a result of the Russian bombings. Vitalii himself lost four friends. He also recounted a story about a man who was killed just riding his bicycle home. At the end of the street where Vitalii lives, a man was shot because he went outside after 10:00 pm.

Until February 24, Vitalii did not believe that this terrible full-scale war could happen. Even when convoys of Russian vehicles were driving nearby, he still did not believe it.

Now Vitalii hates Russians: "I can't even listen to their songs. They are inhuman to me. Why did they do such things in Bucha and Irpin... Why? How many people were killed? For what? For that stupid Putin?"

This text is based on testimony collected by the Kharkiv Human Rights Protection Group.

UKRAINIAN VOICES

Collected by Andreas Umland

1 *Mychailo Wynnyckyj*
  Ukraine's Maidan, Russia's War
  A Chronicle and Analysis of the Revolution of Dignity
  With a foreword by Serhii Plokhy
  ISBN 978-3-8382-1327-9

2 *Olexander Hryb*
  Understanding Contemporary Ukrainian and Russian Nationalism
  The Post-Soviet Cossack Revival and Ukraine's National Security
  With a foreword by Vitali Vitaliev
  ISBN 978-3-8382-1377-4

3 *Marko Bojcun*
  Towards a Political Economy of Ukraine
  Selected Essays 1990–2015
  With a foreword by John-Paul Himka
  ISBN 978-3-8382-1368-2

4 *Volodymyr Yermolenko (ed.)*
  Ukraine in Histories and Stories
  Essays by Ukrainian Intellectuals
  With a preface by Peter Pomerantsev
  ISBN 978-3-8382-1456-6

5 *Mykola Riabchuk*
  At the Fence of Metternich's Garden
  Essays on Europe, Ukraine, and Europeanization
  ISBN 978-3-8382-1484-9

6 *Marta Dyczok*
  Ukraine Calling
  A Kaleidoscope from Hromadske Radio 2016–2019
  With a foreword by Andriy Kulykov
  ISBN 978-3-8382-1472-6

7 *Olexander Scherba*
  Ukraine vs. Darkness
  Undiplomatic Thoughts
  With a foreword by Adrian Karatnycky
  ISBN 978-3-8382-1501-3

8 *Olesya Yaremchuk*
  Our Others
  Stories of Ukrainian Diversity
  With a foreword by Ostap Slyvynsky
  Translated from the Ukrainian by Zenia Tompkins and Hanna Leliv
  ISBN 978-3-8382-1475-7

9 *Nataliya Gumenyuk*
  Die verlorene Insel
  Geschichten von der besetzten Krim
  Mit einem Vorwort von Alice Bota
  Aus dem Ukrainischen übersetzt von Johann Zajaczkowski
  ISBN 978-3-8382-1499-3

10 *Olena Stiazhkina*
   Zero Point Ukraine
   Four Essays on World War II
   Translated from the Ukrainian by Svitlana Kulinska
   ISBN 978-3-8382-1550-1

11 Oleksii Sinchenko, Dmytro Stus, Leonid Finberg (compilers)
    Ukrainian Dissidents
    An Anthology of Texts
    ISBN 978-3-8382-1551-8

12 John-Paul Himka
    Ukrainian Nationalists and the Holocaust
    OUN and UPA's Participation in the Destruction of Ukrainian Jewry, 1941–1944
    ISBN 978-3-8382-1548-8

13 Andrey Demartino
    False Mirrors
    The Weaponization of Social Media in Russia's Operation to Annex Crimea
    With a foreword by Oleksiy Danilov
    ISBN 978-3-8382-1533-4

14 Svitlana Biedarieva (ed.)
    Contemporary Ukrainian and Baltic Art
    Political and Social Perspectives, 1991–2021
    ISBN 978-3-8382-1526-6

15 Olesya Khromeychuk
    A Loss
    The Story of a Dead Soldier Told by His Sister
    With a foreword by Andrey Kurkov
    ISBN 978-3-8382-1570-9

16 Marieluise Beck (Hg.)
    Ukraine verstehen
    Auf den Spuren von Terror und Gewalt
    Mit einem Vorwort von Dmytro Kuleba
    ISBN 978-3-8382-1653-9

17 Stanislav Aseyev
    Heller Weg
    Geschichte eines Konzentrationslagers im Donbass 2017–2019
    Aus dem Russischen übersetzt von Martina Steis und Charis Haska
    ISBN 978-3-8382-1620-1

18 Mykola Davydiuk
    Wie funktioniert Putins Propaganda?
    Anmerkungen zum Informationskrieg des Kremls
    Aus dem Ukrainischen übersetzt von Christian Weise
    ISBN 978-3-8382-1628-7

19 Olesya Yaremchuk
    Unsere Anderen
    Geschichten ukrainischer Vielfalt
    Aus dem Ukrainischen übersetzt von Christian Weise
    ISBN 978-3-8382-1635-5

20 Oleksandr Mykhed
    „Dein Blut wird die Kohle tränken"
    Über die Ostukraine
    Aus dem Ukrainischen übersetzt von Simon Muschick und Dario Planert
    ISBN 978-3-8382-1648-5

21 Vakhtang Kipiani (Hg.)
    Der Zweite Weltkrieg in der Ukraine
    Geschichte und Lebensgeschichten
    Aus dem Ukrainischen übersetzt von Margarita Grinko
    ISBN 978-3-8382-1622-5

22 Vakhtang Kipiani (ed.)
    World War II, Uncontrived and Unredacted
    Testimonies from Ukraine
    Translated from the Ukrainian by Zenia Tompkins and Daisy Gibbons
    ISBN 978-3-8382-1621-8

23 Dmytro Stus
   Vasyl Stus
   Life in Creativity
   Translated from the Ukrainian by
   Ludmila Bachurina
   ISBN 978-3-8382-1631-7

24 Vitalii Ogiienko (ed.)
   The Holodomor and the
   Origins of the Soviet Man
   Reading the Testimony of
   Anastasia Lysyvets
   With forewords by Natalka
   Bilotserkivets and Serhy
   Yekelchyk
   Translated from the Ukrainian by
   Alla Parkhomenko and
   Alexander J. Motyl
   ISBN 978-3-8382-1616-4

25 Vladislav Davidzon
   Jewish-Ukrainian Relations
   and the Birth of a Political
   Nation
   Selected Writings 2013-2021
   With a foreword by Bernard-
   Henri Lévy
   ISBN 978-3-8382-1509-9

26 Serhy Yekelchyk
   Writing the Nation
   The Ukrainian Historical
   Profession in Independent
   Ukraine and the Diaspora
   ISBN 978-3-8382-1695-9

27 Ildi Eperjesi, Oleksandr
   Kachura
   Shreds of War
   Fates from the Donbas Frontline
   2014-2019
   With a foreword by Olexiy
   Haran
   ISBN 978-3-8382-1680-5

28 Oleksandr Melnyk
   World War II as an Identity
   Project
   Historicism, Legitimacy
   Contests, and the (Re-)Con-
   struction of Political Commu-
   nities in Ukraine, 1939–1946
   With a foreword by David R.
   Marples
   ISBN 978-3-8382-1704-8

29 Olesya Khromeychuk
   Ein Verlust
   Die Geschichte eines gefallenen
   ukrainischen Soldaten, erzählt
   von seiner Schwester
   Mit einem Vorwort von Andrej
   Kurkow
   Aus dem Englischen übersetzt
   von Lily Sophie
   ISBN 978-3-8382-1770-3

30 Tamara Martsenyuk,
   Tetiana Kostiuchenko (eds.)
   Russia's War in Ukraine
   During 2022
   Personal Experiences of
   Ukrainian Scholars
   ISBN 978-3-8382-1757-4

31 Ildikó Eperjesi, Oleksandr
   Kachura
   Shreds of War. Vol. 2
   Fates from Crimea 2015–2022
   With an interview of Oleh
   Sentsov
   ISBN 978-3-8382-1780-2

32 Yuriy Lukanov
   The Press
   How Russia Destroyed Media
   Freedom in Crimea
   With a foreword by Taras Kuzio
   ISBN 978-3-8382-1784-0

33 Megan Buskey
   Ukraine Is Not Dead Yet
   A Family Story of Exile and
   Return
   ISBN 978-3-8382-1691-1

34 Vira Ageyeva
Behind the Scenes of the Empire
Essays on Cultural Relationships between Ukraine and Russia
With a foreword by Oksana Zabuzhko
ISBN 978-3-8382-1748-2

35 Marieluise Beck (ed.)
Understanding Ukraine
Tracing the Roots of Terror and Violence
With a foreword by Dmytro Kuleba
ISBN 978-3-8382-1773-4

36 Olesya Khromeychuk
A Loss
The Story of a Dead Soldier Told by His Sister, 2nd edn.
With a foreword by Philippe Sands
With a preface by Andrii Kurkov
ISBN 978-3-8382-1870-0

37 Taras Kuzio, Stefan Jajecznyk-Kelman
Fascism and Genocide
Russia's War Against Ukrainians
ISBN 978-3-8382-1791-8

38 Alina Nychyk
Ukraine Vis-à-Vis Russia and the EU
Misperceptions of Foreign Challenges in Times of War, 2014–2015
With a foreword by Paul D'Anieri
ISBN 978-3-8382-1767-3

39 Sasha Dovzhyk (ed.)
Ukraine Lab
Global Security, Environment, and Disinformation Through the Prism of Ukraine
With a foreword by Rory Finnin
ISBN 978-3-8382-1805-2

40 Serhiy Kvit
Media, History, and Education
Three Ways to Ukrainian Independence
With a preface by Diane Francis
ISBN 978-3-8382-1807-6

41 Anna Romandash
Women of Ukraine
Reportages from the War and Beyond
ISBN 978-3-8382-1819-9

42 Dominika Rank
Matzewe in meinem Garten
Abenteuer eines jüdischen Heritage-Touristen in der Ukraine
ISBN 978-3-8382-1810-6

43 Myroslaw Marynowytsch
Das Universum hinter dem Stacheldraht
Memoiren eines sowjet-ukrainischen Dissidenten
Mit einem Vorwort von Timothy Snyder und einem Nachwort von Max Hartmann
ISBN 978-3-8382-1806-9

44 Konstantin Sigow
Für Deine und meine Freiheit
Europäische Revolutions- und Kriegserfahrungen im heutigen Kyjiw
Mit einem Vorwort von Karl Schlögel
Herausgegeben von Regula M. Zwahlen
ISBN 978-3-8382-1755-0

45 Kateryna Pylypchuk
The War that Changed Us
Ukrainian Novellas, Poems, and Essays from 2022
With a foreword by Victor Yushchenko
Paperback
ISBN 978-3-8382-1859-5
Hardcover
ISBN 978-3-8382-1860-1

46 Kyrylo Tkachenko
   Rechte Tür Links
   Radikale Linke in Deutschland, die Revolution und der Krieg in der Ukraine, 2013-2018
   ISBN 978-3-8382-1711-6

47 Alexander Strashny
   The Ukrainian Mentality
   An Ethno-Psychological, Historical and Comparative Exploration
   With a foreword by Antonina Lovochkina
   Translated from the Ukrainian by Michael M. Naydan and Olha Tytarenko
   ISBN 978-3-8382-1886-1

48 Alona Shestopalova
   From Screens to Battlefields
   Tracing the Construction of Enemies on Russian Television
   With a foreword by Nina Jankowicz
   ISBN 978-3-8382-1884-7

49 Iaroslav Petik
   Politics and Society in the Ukrainian People's Republic (1917–1921) and Contemporary Ukraine (2013–2022)
   A Comparative Analysis
   With a foreword by Mykola Doroshko
   ISBN 978-3-8382-1817-5

50 Serhii Plokhy
   Der Mann mit der Giftpistole
   Eine Spionagechichte aus dem Kalten Krieg
   ISBN 978-3-8382-1789-5

51 Vakhtang Kipiani
   Ukrainische Dissidenten unter der Sowjetmacht
   Im Kampf um Wahrheit und Freiheit
   Aus dem Ukrainischen übersetzt von Christian Weise
   ISBN 978-3-8382-1890-8

52 Dmytro Shestakov
   When Businesses Test Hypotheses
   A Four-Step Approach to Risk Management for Innovative Startups
   With a foreword by Anthony J. Tether
   ISBN 978-3-8382-1883-0

53 Larissa Babij
   A Kind of Refugee
   The Story of an American Who Refused to Leave Ukraine
   With a foreword by Vladislav Davidzon
   ISBN 978-3-8382-1898-4

54 Julia Davis
   In Their Own Words
   How Russian Propagandists Reveal Putin's Intentions
   With a foreword by Timothy Snyder
   ISBN 978-3-8382-1909-7

55 Sonya Atlantova, Oleksandr Klymenko
   Icons on Ammo Boxes
   Painting Life on the Remnants of Russia's War in Donbas, 2014-21
   Translated from the Ukrainian by Anastasya Knyazhytska
   ISBN 978-3-8382-1892-2

56 Leonid Ushkalov
   Catching an Elusive Bird
   The Life of Hryhorii Skovoroda
   Translated from the Ukrainian by Natalia Komarova
   ISBN 978-3-8382-1894-6

57 Vakhtang Kipiani
   Ein Land weiblichen Geschlechts
   Ukrainische Frauenschicksale im 20. und 21. Jahrhundert
   Aus dem Ukrainischen übersetzt von Christian Weise
   ISBN 978-3-8382-1891-5

58 *Petro Rychlo*
   „Zerrissne Saiten einer überlauten Harfe ..."
   Deutschjüdische Dichter der Bukowina
   ISBN 978-3-8382-1893-9

59 *Volodymyr Paniotto*
   Sociology in Jokes
   An Entertaining Introduction
   ISBN 978-3-8382-1857-1

60 *Josef Wallmannsberger (ed.)*
   Executing Renaissances
   The Poetological Nation of Ukraine
   ISBN 978-3-8382-1741-3

61 *Pavlo Kazarin*
   The Wild West of Eastern Europe
   A Ukrainian Guide on Breaking Free from Empire
   Translated from the Ukrainian by Dominique Hoffman
   ISBN 978-3-8382-1842-7

62 *Ernest Gyidel*
   Ukrainian Public Nationalism in the General Government
   The Case of Krakivski Visti, 1940–1944
   With a foreword by David R. Marples
   ISBN 978-3-8382-1865-6

63 *Olexander Hryb*
   Understanding Contemporary Russian Militarism
   From Revolutionary to New Generation Warfare
   With a foreword by Mark Laity
   ISBN 978-3-8382-1927-1

64 *Orysia Hrudka, Bohdan Ben*
   Dark Days, Determined People
   Stories from Ukraine under Siege
   With a foreword by Myroslav Marynovych
   ISBN 978-3-8382-1958-5

65 *Oleksandr Pankieiev (ed.)*
   Narratives of the Russo-Ukrainian War
   A Look Within and Without
   With a foreword by Natalia Khanenko-Friesen
   ISBN 978-3-8382-1964-6

66 *Roman Sohn, Ariana Gic (eds.)*
   Unrecognized War
   The Fight for Truth about Russia's War on Ukraine
   With a foreword by Viktor Yushchenko
   ISBN 978-3-8382-1947-9

67 *Paul Robert Magocsi*
   Ukraina Redux
   Schon wieder die Ukraine ...
   ISBN 978-3-8382-1942-4

68 *Paul Robert Magocsi*
   L'Ucraina Ritrovata
   Sullo Stato e l'Identità Nazionale
   ISBN 978-3-8382-1982-0

69 *Max Hartmann*
   Ein Schrei der Verzweiflung
   Aquarelle zum Krieg von Danylo Movchan
   Paperback
   ISBN 978-3-8382-2011-6
   Hardcover
   ISBN 978-3-8382-2012-3

70 *Vakhtang Kebuladze (Hg.)*
   Die Zukunft, die wir uns wünschen
   Essays aus der Ukraine
   ISBN 978-3-8382-1531-0

71 Marieluise Beck, Jan Claas Behrends, Gelinada Grinchenko und Oksana Mikheieva (Hg.)
Deutsch-ukrainische Geschichten
Bruchstücke aus einer gemeinsamen Vergangenheit
ISBN 978-3-8382-2053-6

72 Pavlo Kazarin
Der Wilde Westen Ost-Europas
Aus dem Ukrainischen übersetzt von Christian Weise
ISBN 978-3-8382-1843-4

73 Radomyr Mokryk
Ukrainian Sixtiers
Against the Empire
ISBN 978-3-8382-1873-1

74 Leonid Finberg
My Ukraine—Rethinking the Past, Building the Present
ISBN 978-3-8382-1974-5

75 Joseph Zissels
Consider My Inmost Thoughts
Texts and Interviews on Ukrainian Matters at the Turn of the Century
ISBN 978-3-8382-1975-2

76 Margarita Yehorchenko, Iryna Berlyand, Ihor Vinokurov (eds.)
Jewish Addresses in Ukraine
A Guide-Book
With a foreword by Leonid Finberg
ISB 978-3-8382-1976-9

77 Viktoriia Grivina
Kharkiv—A War City
A Collection of Essays from 2022–23
ISBN 978-3-8382-1988-2

78 Hjørdis Clemmensen, Viktoriia Grivina, Vasylysa Shchogoleva
Kharkiv Is a Dream
Public Art and Activism 2013–2023
With a foreword by Bohdan Volynskyi
ISBN 978-3-8382-2005-5

79 Olga Khomenko
The Faraway Sky of Kyiv
Ukrainians in the War
With a foreword by Hiroaki Kuromiya
ISBN 978-3-8382-2006-2

80 Daria Mattingly, Jonathon Vsetecka (eds.)
The Holodomor in Global Perspective
How the Famine in Ukraine Shaped the World
ISBN 978-3-8382-1953-0

81 Olga Khomenko
Ukrainians beyond Borders
Nine Life Journeys Through the History of Eastern Europe
With a foreword by Zbigniew Wojnowski
ISBN 978-3-8382-2007-9

82 Mykhailo Minakov
From Servant to Leader
Chronicles of Ukraine under the Zelensky presidency, 2019–2024
ISBN 978-3-8382-2002-4

83 Wolodymyr Hromov (ed.)
A Ruined Home
Sketches of War, 2022–2023
ISBN 978-3-8382-2008-6

84 Olha Tatokhina (ed.)
Why do they kill our people?
Russia's war against Ukraine as told by Ukrainians
ISBN 978-3-8382-2056-7

Book series "Ukrainian Voices"

Coordinator
Andreas Umland, National University of Kyiv-Mohyla Academy

Editorial Board
Lesia Bidochko, National University of Kyiv-Mohyla Academy
Svitlana Biedarieva, George Washington University, DC, USA
Ivan Gomza, Kyiv School of Economics, Ukraine
Natalie Jaresko, Aspen Institute, Kyiv/Washington
Olena Lennon, University of New Haven, West Haven, USA
Kateryna Yushchenko, First Lady of Ukraine 2005-2010, Kyiv
Oleksandr Zabirko, University of Regensburg, Germany

Advisory Board
Iuliia Bentia, National Academy of Arts of Ukraine, Kyiv
Natalya Belitser, Pylyp Orlyk Institute for Democracy, Kyiv
Oleksandra Bienert, Humboldt University of Berlin, Germany
Sergiy Bilenky, Canadian Institute of Ukrainian Studies, Toronto
Tymofii Brik, Kyiv School of Economics, Ukraine
Olga Brusylovska, Mechnikov National University, Odesa
Mariana Budjeryn, Harvard University, Cambridge, USA
Volodymyr Bugrov, Shevchenko National University, Kyiv
Olga Burlyuk, University of Amsterdam, The Netherlands
Yevhen Bystrytsky, NAS Institute of Philosophy, Kyiv
Andrii Danylenko, Pace University, New York, USA
Vladislav Davidzon, Atlantic Council, Washington/Paris
Mykola Davydiuk, Think Tank "Polityka," Kyiv
Andrii Demartino, National Security and Defense Council, Kyiv
Vadym Denisenko, Ukrainian Institute for the Future, Kyiv
Oleksandr Donii, Center for Political Values Studies, Kyiv
Volodymyr Dubovyk, Mechnikov National University, Odesa
Volodymyr Dubrovskiy, CASE Ukraine, Kyiv
Diana Dutsyk, National University of Kyiv-Mohyla Academy
Marta Dyczok, Western University, Ontario, Canada
Yevhen Fedchenko, National University of Kyiv-Mohyla Academy
Sofiya Filonenko, State Pedagogical University of Berdyansk
Oleksandr Fisun, Karazin National University, Kharkiv
Oksana Forostyna, Webjournal "Ukraina Moderna," Kyiv
Roman Goncharenko, Broadcaster "Deutsche Welle," Bonn
George Grabowicz, Harvard University, Cambridge, USA
Gelinada Grinchenko, Karazin National University, Kharkiv
Kateryna Härtel, Federal Union of European Nationalities, Brussels
Nataliia Hendel, University of Geneva, Switzerland
Anton Herashchenko, Kyiv School of Public Administration
John-Paul Himka, University of Alberta, Edmonton
Ola Hnatiuk, National University of Kyiv-Mohyla Academy
Oleksandr Holubov, Broadcaster "Deutsche Welle," Bonn
Yaroslav Hrytsak, Ukrainian Catholic University, Lviv
Oleksandra Humenna, National University of Kyiv-Mohyla Academy
Tamara Hundorova, NAS Institute of Literature, Kyiv
Oksana Huss, University of Bologna, Italy
Oleksandra Iwaniuk, University of Warsaw, Poland
Mykola Kapitonenko, Shevchenko National University, Kyiv
Georgiy Kasianov, Marie Curie-Skłodowska University, Lublin
Vakhtang Kebuladze, Shevchenko National University, Kyiv
Natalia Khanenko-Friesen, University of Alberta, Edmonton
Victoria Khiterer, Millersville University of Pennsylvania, USA
Oksana Kis, NAS Institute of Ethnology, Lviv
Pavlo Klimkin, Center for National Resilience and Development, Kyiv
Oleksandra Kolomiiets, Center for Economic Strategy, Kyiv

Sergiy Korsunsky, Kobe Gakuin University, Japan
Nadiia Koval, Kyiv School of Economics, Ukraine
Volodymyr Kravchenko, University of Alberta, Edmonton
Oleksiy Kresin, NAS Koretskiy Institute of State and Law, Kyiv
Anatoliy Kruglashov, Fedkovych National University, Chernivtsi
Andrey Kurkov, PEN Ukraine, Kyiv
Ostap Kushnir, Lazarski University, Warsaw
Taras Kuzio, National University of Kyiv-Mohyla Academy
Serhii Kvit, National University of Kyiv-Mohyla Academy
Yuliya Ladygina, The Pennsylvania State University, USA
Yevhen Mahda, Institute of World Policy, Kyiv
Victoria Malko, California State University, Fresno, USA
Yulia Marushevska, Security and Defense Center (SAND), Kyiv
Myroslav Marynovych, Ukrainian Catholic University, Lviv
Oleksandra Matviichuk, Center for Civil Liberties, Kyiv
Mykhailo Minakov, Kennan Institute, Washington, USA
Anton Moiseienko, The Australian National University, Canberra
Alexander Motyl, Rutgers University-Newark, USA
Vlad Mykhnenko, University of Oxford, United Kingdom
Vitalii Ogiienko, Ukrainian Institute of National Remembrance, Kyiv
Olga Onuch, University of Manchester, United Kingdom
Olesya Ostrovska, Museum "Mystetskyi Arsenal," Kyiv
Anna Osypchuk, National University of Kyiv-Mohyla Academy
Oleksandr Pankieiev, University of Alberta, Edmonton
Oleksiy Panych, Publishing House "Dukh i Litera," Kyiv
Valerii Pekar, Kyiv-Mohyla Business School, Ukraine
Yohanan Petrovsky-Shtern, Northwestern University, Chicago
Serhii Plokhy, Harvard University, Cambridge, USA
Andrii Portnov, Viadrina University, Frankfurt-Oder, Germany
Maryna Rabinovych, Kyiv School of Economics, Ukraine
Valentyna Romanova, Institute of Developing Economies, Tokyo
Natalya Ryabinska, Collegium Civitas, Warsaw, Poland
Darya Tsymbalyk, University of Oxford, United Kingdom
Vsevolod Samokhvalov, University of Liege, Belgium
Orest Semotiuk, Franko National University, Lviv
Viktoriya Sereda, NAS Institute of Ethnology, Lviv
Anton Shekhovtsov, University of Vienna, Austria
Andriy Shevchenko, Media Center Ukraine, Kyiv
Oxana Shevel, Tufts University, Medford, USA
Pavlo Shopin, National Pedagogical Dragomanov University, Kyiv
Karina Shyrokykh, Stockholm University, Sweden
Nadja Simon, freelance interpreter, Cologne, Germany
Olena Snigova, NAS Institute for Economics and Forecasting, Kyiv
Ilona Solohub, Analytical Platform "VoxUkraine," Kyiv
Iryna Solonenko, LibMod - Center for Liberal Modernity, Berlin
Galyna Solovei, National University of Kyiv-Mohyla Academy
Sergiy Stelmakh, NAS Institute of World History, Kyiv
Olena Stiazhkina, NAS Institute of the History of Ukraine, Kyiv
Dmitri Stratievski, Osteuropa Zentrum (OEZB), Berlin
Dmytro Stus, National Taras Shevchenko Museum, Kyiv
Frank Sysyn, University of Toronto, Canada
Olha Tokariuk, Center for European Policy Analysis, Washington
Olena Tregub, Independent Anti-Corruption Commission, Kyiv
Hlib Vyshlinsky, Centre for Economic Strategy, Kyiv
Mychailo Wynnyckyj, National University of Kyiv-Mohyla Academy
Yelyzaveta Yasko, NGO "Yellow Blue Strategy," Kyiv
Serhy Yekelchyk, University of Victoria, Canada
Victor Yushchenko, President of Ukraine 2005-2010, Kyiv
Oleksandr Zaitsev, Ukrainian Catholic University, Lviv
Kateryna Zarembo, National University of Kyiv-Mohyla Academy
Yaroslav Zhalilo, National Institute for Strategic Studies, Kyiv
Sergei Zhuk, Ball State University at Muncie, USA
Alina Zubkovych, Nordic Ukraine Forum, Stockholm
Liudmyla Zubrytska, National University of Kyiv-Mohyla Academy

Friends of the Series

Ana Maria Abulescu, University of Bucharest, Romania
Łukasz Adamski, Centrum Mieroszewskiego, Warsaw
Marieluise Beck, LibMod—Center for Liberal Modernity, Berlin
Marc Berensen, King's College London, United Kingdom
Johannes Bohnen, BOHNEN Public Affairs, Berlin
Karsten Brüggemann, University of Tallinn, Estonia
Ulf Brunnbauer, Leibniz Institute (IOS), Regensburg
Martin Dietze, German-Ukrainian Culture Society, Hamburg
Gergana Dimova, Florida State University, Tallahassee/London
Caroline von Gall, Goethe University, Frankfurt-Main
Zaur Gasimov, Rhenish Friedrich Wilhelm University, Bonn
Armand Gosu, University of Bucharest, Romania
Thomas Grant, University of Cambridge, United Kingdom
Gustav Gressel, European Council on Foreign Relations, Berlin
Rebecca Harms, European Centre for Press & Media Freedom, Leipzig
André Härtel, Stiftung Wissenschaft und Politik, Berlin/Brussels
Marcel Van Herpen, The Cicero Foundation, Maastricht
Richard Herzinger, freelance analyst, Berlin
Mieste Hotopp-Riecke, ICATAT, Magdeburg
Nico Lange, Munich Security Conference, Berlin
Martin Malek, freelance analyst, Vienna
Ingo Mannteufel, Broadcaster "Deutsche Welle," Bonn
Carlo Masala, Bundeswehr University, Munich
Wolfgang Mueller, University of Vienna, Austria
Dietmar Neutatz, Albert Ludwigs University, Freiburg
Torsten Oppelland, Friedrich Schiller University, Jena
Niccolò Pianciola, University of Padua, Italy
Gerald Praschl, German-Ukrainian Forum (DUF), Berlin
Felix Riefer, Think Tank Ideenagentur-Ost, Düsseldorf
Stefan Rohdewald, University of Leipzig, Germany
Sebastian Schäffer, Institute for the Danube Region (IDM), Vienna
Felix Schimansky-Geier, Friedrich Schiller University, Jena
Ulrich Schneckener, University of Osnabrück, Germany
Winfried Schneider-Deters, freelance analyst, Heidelberg/Kyiv
Gerhard Simon, University of Cologne, Germany
Kai Struve, Martin Luther University, Halle/Wittenberg
David Stulik, European Values Center for Security Policy, Prague
Andrzej Szeptycki, University of Warsaw, Poland
Philipp Ther, University of Vienna, Austria
Stefan Troebst, University of Leipzig, Germany

[Please send requests for changes in, corrections of, and additions to, this list to andreas.umland@stanforalumni.org.]

ibidem.eu